CARRYING OVER

T0151945

Carrying Over

Carolyn Kizer

POEMS FROM THE CHINESE,

URDU, MACEDONIAN,

YIDDISH, AND FRENCH AFRICAN

COPPER CANYON PRESS

Poems and translations from *Carrying Over* have appeared in *Choice, The Hudson Review, Kayak, The Nation, Tar River, The St. Andrews Review, Ironwood,* and *Delos.*

The two poems by Rachel Korn were translated for *A Treasury of Yiddish Poetry,* edited by Irving Howe and Eliezer Greenberg (Holt, Rinehart & Winston).

"The Pakistan Journal" appeared in *The Hudson Review.*

Translations of Tu Fu appeared in *Knock Upon Silence* (University of Washington Press).

Six translations of Macedonian poems appeared in the anthology, *Reading the Ashes,* edited by Milne Holton and Graham W. Reid (Pittsburgh).

The translation of Edouard J. Maunick's "Sept Versants Sept Syllables" was first printed in *Poetry Magazine,* and subsequently appeared in Ellen Conroy Kennedy's *The Negritude Poets* (Viking).

Shu Ting's poems, "Missing" and "To the Oak" also appeared in *Poetry Magazine.*

SECOND PRINTING
ISBN 1-55659-016-4 (cloth)
ISBN 1-55659-017-2 (paper)
Library of Congress Card Number 88-070586

The cover is "A Barge Scene on the River" by Sin Yun-bok (mid-18th century), from the Kansong Museum.

The publication of this book was supported by a grant from the National Endowment for the Arts. Copper Canyon Press is in residence with Centrum at Fort Worden State Park.

COPPER CANYON PRESS
P.O. Box 271, Port Townsend, WA 98368

FOR

MIKE KEELEY

DONALD KEENE

WILLIAM MERWIN

III. Pakistan

A JOURNAL AND POEMS BY THREE POETS

IV. Yugoslavia

A PROSE POEM ON TRANSLATION, AND
NINE TRANSLATIONS FROM THE MACEDONIAN

V. African Presence

A TRANSLATION FROM THE FRENCH OF
EDOUARD MAUNICK AND A POEM

VI. New China

SHU TING: A POEM IN SIXTEEN SECTIONS
AND TEN OTHER POEMS

Introduction

Unlike the distinguished friends to whom this book is dedicated, I am only an occasional and amateur translator. Though I retain a few phrases of kitchen and tourist French, Urdu and Chinese, I speak only enough Macedonian to order plum brandy. I know those useful words of Yiddish employed by many American gentiles of my generation who were raised by radio, by Jack Benny in particular, and further educated by Norman Rosten – words and phrases that have no equivalent in English. Furthermore, I have not, as my friends have, translated the entire body of work of a given period or a given author.

Prompted by Donald Keene and assisted by Cyril Birch, I have 'translated' more poems from the T'ang Dynasty, particularly those of Tu Fu, than from any other source. My interest in Chinese poetry is passionate, and of long standing. Mother read me the translations of Arthur Waley beginning when I was around eight; in due course, I wrote my college thesis on the influence of Chinese poetry in translation on the Imagists (and, by reference, me). Upon graduating from Sarah Lawrence, I took up a Chinese Cultural Fellowship in Comparative Literature at Columbia University, interrupted by the chance to go to China, where my father was administering United Nations relief. Most of the Chinese I learned from dear Professor Carrington Goodrich at Columbia and spoke in Peking afterwards has slipped away. For years I flattered myself that I could still use Matthews' great Chinese Dictionary, but now I read it only for pleasure and enlightenment.

The two poems translated from the Yiddish of Rachel Korn were commissioned by Irving Howe who, with Eliezer Greenberg, edited *A Treasury of Yiddish Poetry* (Holt, Rinehart & Winston). Mr. Howe sent me a tape of her poems in Yiddish, along with a prose crib; then my versions were carefully checked by the editors. I later had the great pleasure of reading with Rachel Korn at the YMHA in New York, along with other Yiddish poets and their translators. After the terrible background of the Holocaust from which these few emerged, I expected to see a group of crumbling and broken men and women. I "dressed down" for the occasion, as they say. What joy, then, to be instantly eclipsed by Ms. Korn, an erect and handsome woman in a glittering gold dress with sable cuffs!

I spent the academic year 1964–1965 in Pakistan, where I became
acquainted with a number of poets, and returned for a meeting of the
M.L.A. in 1969. Before I left in 1964, I met the late N. M. Rashid,
then Pakistan's Ambassador to the United Nations, and translated the
poem included here with him. My late friend, James Wright, has
translated a number of Rashid's poems. I met Faiz Ahmad Faiz in
Pakistan – Faiz, the greatest Urdu poet of the sub-continent (now
ably and extensively translated by my friend, Naomi Lazard). More
about Faiz is included in the Journal that is printed here. An early
draft of Faiz's poem, "If I Were Certain," was composed with the help
of Mohammad Sarfaraz, of the Pakistani United Nations delegation,
in New York, and later gone over with the author, as were the other
poems of Faiz included here. Faiz died in Lahore in the autumn of
1984, making this a sadly mortuary paragraph.

My "Pakistan Journal" appears in this volume because it sheds
some light on the background from which these poems spring, and
because I think it is still amusing to read. Little has changed in the
eighteen years since it was written, and nothing has changed for the
better, an opinion reinforced by friends who live there now or have
visited recently. Would I go back again, despite wars, dictators, refu-
gees, the oppression of women, the wistfulness of men? Like a shot.

I have been to Macedonian Yugoslavia a number of times to attend
the Struga Festival, and early on formed a fast friendship with the
poet and playwright, Bogomil Gjuzel. Our translations of his work
are a collaboration, as are those of the poets Mateja Matevski and
Radovan Pavlovski. (Anté Popovski's poem was translated from the
French with the help of my husband, John Woodbridge.) There exists
an hilarious tape of Bogomil and me, translating. Excerpt: Bogomil:
You understand what I mean by erection? Upright pennies? Me:
Upright *pennies*? You mean like when we were children and put them
on the railroad track so the train would flatten them? Bogomil (total
consternation)!!! Me (total lack of communication)??? Bogomil: No,
fool! *Pennies!* COCK!

Versions of Macedonian poems were originally solicited by Milne
Holton and Graham W. Reid for their anthology of Modern Mace-
donian poems, *Reading the Ashes* (Pittsburgh).

I wrote the poem "Race Relations" for my courageous South African
friend, the exiled Dennis Brutus. At a poetry festival in Rotterdam

one year, we poets wrote poems to each other and stuck them in one another's mailboxes at the hotel: this poem was one of those, as is the prose-poem to Lars Gustafsson at the beginning of the Macedonian section. What a lovely time.

The Edouard Maunick poem was translated with the author on a memorable visit of his to Washington, D.C. When not translating he cooked, magnificently. (I've been trying to duplicate a sort of ratatouille with chicken that he made, ever since.) I especially remember one translation session around a friend's swimming pool beginning about ten in the morning. Suddenly I noticed we were both shivering. Night had fallen.

To quote from Ellen Kennedy in her book, *The Negritude Poets* (Viking), "Edouard Maunick comes from a volcanic dot 720 miles square that lies west of Madagascar, midway between Africa and India": Mauritius. He is a mixture of French, African and Irish blood. Mrs. Kennedy goes on to say that "Miss Kizer accomplishes the difficult technical feat of duplicating the seven-syllable lines with which Maunick composed his poem. His powerful imagery is intact, along with the challenging syntax." Which is why I include the French here, so that some of you can compare for yourselves. "Seven Sides and Seven Syllables" was translated for Mrs. Kennedy's book, but appeared first in *Poetry* magazine.

Shu Ting, by far the youngest of the poets included here, younger, in fact, than my youngest child (an odd feeling for the translator!), was born in 1952. When the Cultural Revolution swept China in 1966, she was a school-girl of 14; nevertheless, she was rusticated, and in a mountain village far from her home she lived as a peasant. Under these difficult circumstances, reflected by implication in many of her poems, she began to write. None of her poems were allowed in print until 1978, although they circulated from hand to hand; what the Russians call *samisdat*, the Chinese call *di xia wen xue*. When the well-known Peking Spring arrived, she attracted enormous attention, and only a year after her first published poem she won the National Award for Poetry. I've had the pleasure of touring with her and giving bilingual readings. Her charm and dry wit shine right through the language barrier. For example, at a gathering in Santa Cruz, to which all the local writers were invited – many of whom looked as if they had emerged, blinking, from the woods, after two decades of hippiedom – she was asked what influence Zen Buddhism had had on her poetry. Her answer was that she had been more influenced by Christianity. I wish you could have seen their faces. I was introduced to her work by Y. H. Zhao, then earning his graduate degree at Berkeley. He wanted to do an anthology of contemporary Chinese women poets, an idea that attracted me very much. However, I found that only Shu Ting really appealed to me. So Mr. Zhao and I went to work, with the results you find here.

The tone of this introduction – up to this point where I allow Mrs. Kennedy to pat me on the back – has been pretty self-deprecating. Why then, you may well ask, with these shaky credentials, do I have the nerve to put this collection together? Partly it's the instinct I share with the bower-bird: to pile along my path a heap of glittering objects that have attracted me. Partly it's the herding instinct of a sheep-dog: to round up a number of my friends in a tight circle. Partly it's because some people have admired one piece or another, and complained because they were hard to get hold of. But mostly because this potpourri of white Slav and black African, Chinese, Muslim, and Jew, is a kind of paradigm of our world as I wish it were, of the United Nations as I pray it might become: all of us, with sharply individual voices, but together – an orchestra!

Carolyn Kizer
BERKELEY, 1988

I

China

POEMS BY TU FU

(712–770)

Déjeuner sur l'herbe

I

It's pleasant to board the ferry in the sunscape
As the late light slants into afternoon;
The faint wind ruffles the river, rimmed with foam.
We move through the aisles of bamboo
Towards the cool water-lilies.

The young dandies drop ice into the drinks,
While the girls slice the succulent lotus root.
Above us, a patch of cloud spreads, darkening
Like a water-stain on silk.

Write this down quickly, before the rain!

II

Don't sit there! The cushions were soaked by the shower.
Already the girls have drenched their crimson skirts.
Beauties, their powder streaked with mascara,
                lament their ruined faces.

The wind batters our boat, the mooring-line
Has rubbed a wound in the willow bark.
The edges of the curtains are embroidered by river foam.
Like a knife in a melon, Autumn slices Summer.

It will be cold, going back.

Lo Yu Park

freely adapted

An opulent park: serene, we chose the heights.
    Here the horizon fades
        And the bright grass goes on forever. . . .

Our hosts move consciously, aware they create the view,
    themselves the foreground.
Aristocratic, darkly groomed: forms disposed on emerald lawns.
Distant rivers, flat and shiny as freshly-painted landscape
    flow into the ladies' shoulders,
Emerge like scarves the other side.
Sport with the women! Open the lavish hampers!
Guzzle the wine, gleaming and wet as rivers. . . .

Later, half-drunk, slung into saddles,
We are the slaves of horses that gallop away.
Passing the Princess' Pond, we lean over fondly,
Find Spring's young green reflection sobering.
Then, battered by drums from the covered passageway,
We move on.

        The sun is free to enter the Palace yard.
The gate spreads wide, lured open by the sun.
There, where the river curls, we meet the chariots
Sun-plated in silver, moons below the sky.

Blinded by polished gleam, we are distracted
By dancers: their long sleeves dip towards the water.
Courting the water, their skirts tease.
Distracted, distracted: focus our concentration
On a song:
       the singer's voice a thin wire spiraling
To the clouds. . . .

I always get drunk this time of year.
Spring and her melancholy – but now it's too long
Until the wine takes hold. I become so morose!
One doesn't achieve the pleasure any more,
Just the stupidity.
                    I query a half-draped girl:
Who could want this poor pedant with thin hair?
Not the Court, surely. God alone feeds me.
She is tawny from sun, she is half-turned away.
Other bodies recumbent: "Who cares for you?"
I don't mind how drunk I get. I'll take every dare,
Every forfeit. But I can't see beyond the party's end!
Stand alone in the landscape, a sanguine figure.

You, poet, make a song by yourself. Be lost in your song.

The Meandering River Poems

RAIN THERE

Spring clouds rest on the walls of the Royal Park.
Dusk mutes the passionate coloring of blossoms.
Enclosed by the forest, in the River Pavilion,
I look at painted petals, dark from rain.

The wind has extended the waterweeds
Into long, writhing forms:
Like girdles of pale jade, they are curling,
Uncurling on the surface of the stream.

Incense burns in the Hibiscus Hall,
The scent faint, to no purpose,
Where, then, is the irresistible chariot
Guarded by dragons and Imperial tigers?

O King, return! Be liberal with your money!
Revive those elegant Royal entertainments
So I may doze, my old head tilted back
Against a tipsy old brocaded wall

While suave, accomplished ladies
Pluck at my sleeve, as they touch painted lutes.
Or let the prettiest ones
Coax me half-awake. . . .

DRINKING WITH FRIENDS

Tall marsh fowl stalk through the shallows
As little birds nag at the willow buds;

A few wild ducks: puce patterns on gold ground.
Sand on the riverbank is dry and bright

Like our eyes, dry and bright
My friends, our dry, white years!

Eternal yellow sand and sparse white hair,
I ask you what they have to do with Spring?

They come together in the wine-jar, where
We worship all that blooms, all that smells sweet.

Our families? We are bonded to the Court.
The Emperor is our wife, our work, our home.

Ah, we are dry and brilliant, old but strong!
Could *you* learn to seed a furrow, and be free?

DRINKING THERE ALONE

I perch on the riverbank, forgetting to go back,
Gaze down at the lucent palaces as they slip their moorings.
Another pleasant blur – peach-blossoms, redolent
Of bees and heat, compete with willow blooms:
Which will faint first?
                 Birds, white and tawny,
Stripe their migrations, warp
And weft of one another's flight.

Abandon me! But leave me a single swallow
And another. And one more. Dear wine, I don't care!
Abandon me, all of you. This world does not suit;
Not a court regular, unfitted for routine. . . .
Well, well, I am demoted, and my dreams also.
I may no longer look forward to Paradise:
The immortal pleasure of being left alone!
For I summoned, too late, my lost young self
When decision was obsolete.

SPRING GOES

Petal by petal, the Spring dissolves.
A small wind carries the rest away.
All nature conspires to sadden me,
But gross, unrepentant, I will be gay.

I devour the flowers that yet remain.
I shall not stint myself on wine.
A cock, red-throated, a green-winged hen:
The kingfishers nest in the ruined vine.

The River Pavilion lists in decay.
Beyond these boundaries I see
A grave stone unicorn, adamant;
He leans on a tomb, stares far away.

You natural laws! I take your measure;
Forgetting rank, work, weary days.
I find my nature made for pleasure,
And drink and linger, all at ease.

I GO TOO

Each day when Court is over, I skip to the pawnshop,
My nice Spring wardrobe underneath my arm.
Bit by bit, I am drinking up my clothes!
At night I return from the riverbank, quite soused.

Trying not to glance in the taverns – I owe them all –
Slipping past, I reflect on the shortness of life
Especially mine. I'll never see seventy now.
Well, not many do. Who wants to, anyhow?

Saffron butterflies browse deep in flowers;
Dragonflies dint the placid water now and then.
Soothe me, Spring wind! Keep me gentle forever!
Never cross-grained, as Light and Time pass over.

Thwarted

Thwarted, old friend! Here we are, baulked again!
We live at opposite ends of the same lane
But we haven't seen each other for ten whole days.

I returned my Official Horse to the local authorities;
And this road is rotten, like a deliberate plot,
An obstacle race! Now, thanks to my lack of credit

I can't even rent a conveyance, though I still have shoes.
But what if my department-heads caught me afoot?
Taking such risks with protocol, face, future!
You know I'd walk through brambles to get to you.

               *   *   *

By morning the rain is furious. I'm resigned.
The Spring wind raves as I do, in my sleep.
But I'm deaf to the ring-bell and the bang-drum,
The summons to Court. Next door a lame donkey grazes.

A complaisant neighbor owns him, lends him. Ho!
But I daren't ride the beast in the slick mud,
Not to that slippery Palace! Let them mark me absent.
Life is one long, fragmented, murky episode.

               *   *   *

I hate getting through the day without a word;
When you hum your heavenly poems I brim with awe,
Nostalgia at the thought of your sweet cadence.

Magnolia petals fall when they have bloomed,
But you and I are overripe, my friend!
How many times have we two not complained

At the high cost of drinking! Even the corner vendor
Puts too high a price on our Illumination.
We can't steep ourselves in Oblivion any more.

High-sounding, isn't it? Come quickly, then,
To my place, for now it just so happens
I've saved enough small change to buy a gallon.

Adviser to the Court

EAST OF THE PALACE GATES: WORKING LATE

By the water-clock it's past dawn as the day watch sounds.
Spring banners are being unfurled for the morning procession.

Officials march back and forth from the Emperor's audience;
Coming away, we break ranks, to wander among the blossoms.

I turn back towards my office: willow fronds brush my face
As if to veil my yawns. Eyes blurred in the morning mist.

The city walls are moist from snow that has melted
From the high spires. O the fresh odor of wet stone!

Clouds drift among the towers. Alone again,
I burn the draft of another memorandum.

The next time I lift my head I see twilight outside,
Dawn and dusk identical. Time for home, I suppose.

As I amble along on my horse, I hear sleepy cluckings,
The rustle of hay. The chickens are settling down.

TO A BROTHER OFFICIAL

Sound of the fifth watch! Dawn hastens to obey
The water-clock. Officially, day has begun.
Peach blossoms, bibulous and blushing
From spring wine; on the banners
The embroidery dragons move uneasily
As if warmed into life by the new sun.

High above the Palace, swallows dip
In the light breeze. As you hurry from the audience
The odor of incense lingers in your sleeves.
O your crystalline mind, my friend!
You move as lyrically, as rapidly
As you write poems.

Because we honor two talented generations,
Your father and you, we call your offices
West of the Palace Gate, the Phoenix Pond.

WORKING ALL NIGHT IN SPRINGTIME

When day begins to darken,
Flowers along the wall
Merge into the shadows.
Skyward, the birds chirp softly,
Searching for a roost.

Ten thousand common households
Are illumined by the stars,
But the firmament of Heaven
Is soaking up the moonlight
Of this most brilliant night.

So quiet! I hear keys turning
In gold locks of the Palace doors.
The wind a faint jingle, sounding
Like the horses of importuners,
As they shake their pendants of jade.

I must present a memorial
To the Throne-room, in the morning.
Sleepless here, whether I work or not,
All night I measure the hours
Of all night, in my mind. . . .

END OF AN AUDIENCE

Their sleeves like purple orchids
Two ladies of the Court stand by the inner door
of the Throne-room, ushering courtiers from the chamber.
Incense whirls in the hallways – the spring wind!
Sun sparks on the flowered robes of a thousand officials.

The water-clock in the tower shows the hour.
I stand close enough to the Prince to see his expression:
His Majesty looks brilliant with joy today!
When I leave the Palace, I collect my colleagues,
Then we pay our respects to the Ministers of State.

REPLY TO A FRIEND'S ADVICE

Leaving the audience by the quiet corridors,
Stately and beautiful, we pass through the Palace gates,

Turning in different directions: you go to the West
With the Ministers of State. I, otherwise.

On my side, the willow-twigs are fragile, greening.
You are struck by scarlet flowers over there.

Our separate ways! You write so well, so kindly,
To caution, in vain, a garrulous old man.

ON THE WAY OUT

Last year I rejoined the Emperor by this road
When the barbarians swarmed over the Western suburbs.
I'm so far from having recovered from my fear
That shreds of my soul still dangle in the air.

Dangling and wandering, as I am now,
Loyal to the Throne, yet driven away
To a vast, distant province! – surely his Majesty
Could not have intended this. I have been betrayed.

Ruin! As my talent fails, and I grow old.
My steadfastness in trying times has aged me.
I pull on my horse's reins, and, pausing,
Gaze for a final time on the Palace walls.

Banishment

TOO MUCH HEAT, TOO MUCH WORK

It's the fourteenth of August, and I'm too hot
To endure food, or bed. Steam and the fear of scorpions
Keep me awake. I'm told the heat won't fade with Autumn.

Swarms of flies arrive. I'm roped into my clothes.
In another moment I'll scream down the office
As the paper mountains rise higher on my desk.

O those real mountains to the south of here!
I gaze at the ravines kept cool by pines.
If I could walk on ice, with my feet bare!

REUNION

Joy in this meeting grieves our two white heads
Knowing they greet each other a final time.
We nod through the long night watches, still resenting
The speed with which the candle shrinks and pales.

I dread the hour the Milky Way dries up forever.
Let us fill our cups and drain them, over and over
While we can, before the world returns with dawn
When we blot our eyes, and turn our backs on each other.

A Visit in Winter to the Temple of His Mystical Majesty

(Formerly known as The Grand Infinitesimal Palace)

Pole star and northern capital: equal as scepter and orb.
Fences march up the hill like troops protecting the city.
The officer-priests are severe, the guards grim and cautious.

The sky of early winter, celadon, not ice-blue,
Matches the roof-tiles which repel the cold.
Sound of a slap! War between tiles and the weather.

All things come together: In the yard, the gilded tower
Celebrates oneness. Doors, painted with mountains and rivers
Merge with the true landscape, which supports them.

Artifice! To concoct realities, reorder the minute universe,
These roof-beams carved with infinite skill
So that the sun and moon revolve around this place.

The deathless plum-tree has tenacious roots,
Strong as the scent of orchids, sturdy as dynasties.
The victim of history, our Emperor, master of virtue.

When we toll the names of great painters, begin with Wu
Who moved whole countrysides into this room,
Nourished to gleaming life, in a hot-house for Heaven and Earth.

Five learnèd men, in procession like elephants,
Heavy, gray, never breaking their close-linked chain;
Then an orderly flight of geese: a thousand pale officials

Follow them, tame civil servants in dragon robes.
The tassels on their ceremonial head-gear
Toss like flames; wind whips the triangular banners.

Great cedars cast their shadows across the temple grounds
In dark diagonals. Pears, early gold, blush now from the frost.
Hidden by shadows, jade wind-bells move in the eaves:

Their music. The naked, frozen windlass on the well;
Like the silver Emperor of Han, immobilized
For a while. The spirit thaws as the old beliefs are revived.

But is the spirit of man hollow as the note of wind-bells,
Or as a great tree, ripe for felling? Indeed, if we are deathless,
Where then is randomness, Art's impulse, true disorder?

Testament

100 lines from Tu Fu

I come from Tu Ling, an unimportant man,
Only more vulnerable as the years wear on.
To serve my country! I've clung to this mad dream
Without avail, as better men have done.

I bow to hardship whitening my hair,
Old, already spent at forty, I don't care.
When they slam my coffin-lid I shall stay down.
Till then, I will persist, I will endure!

I mourn for my poor people, laboring,
Starving all seasons – I rail against their wrongs.
Though my cloistered fellow-scholars laugh at me
I shall go on pouring out my passionate songs.

I must cleave to the center of life, not the edge of a dream,
Stay with my brilliant Prince, deep in the living stream.
How could one such as I say goodbye to life forever?
Architects, all we need to build a world is here!

                    *   *   *

I have cherished dreams of living by the river;
Spindrift days in sun, without a care.
As clover and sunflower lean toward the source of light
I exult in selfhood, assent to my own spirit.

Any infinitesimal ant wants its own burrow.
Why try to be a whale, prey to great waves or the undertow?
Though I learn my own limitations, I can't learn to obey!
Leave me here on earth, to fail again tomorrow.

When I am silent dust, I will persevere.
To emulate the hermit in his cell,

Relinquishing all! I envy his self-control
And drink uncontrollably to celebrate his call.

I will endure, then thud to earth like a bird
Stricken, to the eternal dust. I will persevere!
So I soothe myself by pouring out the wine
And pouring out my grieved and passionate song.

*   *   *

I find the grasses dying with the year.
Wind rips open the hedge-rows; the thoroughfare
From the capital is black when I start out,
Midnight at my back – I, perpetual traveler!

I cannot tie my coat, the frost is so severe;
Intractable buckles, and fingers stiff with hoar.
The icy sun arises. Troops on the chill frontier
Gather their spears and banners against the invader.

Armies have trampled this ground so many times
Crags are worn smooth; but music fills the ravines!
I arrive at the Mountains of Li with the morning watch.
Beside the sulfur springs is the Emperor's coach.

A gust of steam smokes in the frigid air.
Echoes of bells and drums and resonant cries!
Soaking voluptuously in the opaque jasper waters
The Imperial ministers loll here, take their ease.

*   *   *

The humble and poor are excluded, all their ilk,
Though they are permitted to weave the pure white silk
For the Imperial harem; women full of fear,
Their husbands flogged by greedy courtiers

To extort their exorbitant taxes. Yes, collect the skins
Of miserable men! That's how you serve your King.
Benevolent talents, beware! You will be done in.
It isn't enough simply to love your fellow-man.

What happened to the gold plate on which we used to dine?
Now it decks the boards of the Emperor's rich hangers-on.
But women like goddesses move through the corridors,
Borne on a perfumed wave and swathed in furs.

Incense! You will hear the pensive harp and lute,
Sup on camel-pad broth and nibble rare winter fruit:
Frosty oranges, and little pungent tangerines,
They glow in the hand against warm sable sheens.

When you've gorged, let the wine sour, food to carrion rot!
Fling the meat and drink out of the lacquered gates!
Outside, only steps from plenty, men lie down
To starve, the courtyards littered with their bones.

The span of a woman's arm separates the gilded pillars
Of the Palace from old posts rotten with wind and rain.
On the wild roads the sons of Han lie frozen,
And I, the courtier, freeze with unappeasable pain.

*   *   *

So my traces turn to the North, where two streams meet.
I find the ferry-boat moored at another spot.
The western skies dumped lakes upon the land;
Flood-waters rise to meet my outstretched hand.

Is this wet retribution? Will Heaven's Pillars crack?
A myriad river bridges have swept to rack.
One creaking span remains. We travelers crawl across,
Hand clutching hand. Wide river, hear our curse!

In an evil time, I left my wife in a strange house
Remote from the Court. Now I rejoin my spouse.
I'd rather starve at home than feast at Court.
My Beloveds, I have come to share your fate.

I open my door to wailing. In anguish and anger
My cries join theirs: my infant son has died of hunger.
Even the casual neighbors weep, why not a father?
His guardian, useless and broken, ashamed forever.

My own little child has starved, while I wasn't aware
That our fine autumn harvest had made no difference here.
Dear family, we belong to the privileged class.
How then do the poor endure, starved and harassed

Their property seized, themselves dragged off in bonds
To guard a garrison thousands of miles from home?
What of my life, who have never paid a tax,
Hefted a spear, manned a frontier, beaten a drum?

Our land in flood, and my own heart in flood,
These frantic thoughts are rising like the waters
To flow towards you, wounded, oppressed, bereaved,
In desperate love, China, your sons and daughters.

II

Two Poems from the Yiddish

BY RACHEL H. KORN

Keep Hidden from Me

Keep from me all that I might comprehend!
O God, I ripen toward you in my unknowing.

The barely burgeoning leaf on the roadside tree
Limns innocence: here endeth the first lesson.

Keep from me, God, all forms of certainty:
The steady tread that paces off the self

And forms it, seamless, ignorant of doubt
Or failure, hell-bent for fulfillment.

To know myself: Is that not the supreme disaster?
To know Thee, one must sink on trembling knees.

To hear Thee, only the terrified heart may truly listen;
To see Thee, only the gaze half-blind with dread.

Though the day darken, preserve my memory
From Your bright oblivion. Erase not my faulty traces.

If I aspire again to make four poor walls my house,
Let me pillow myself on the book of my peregrinations.

God, grant me strength to give over false happiness,
And the sense that suffering has earned us Your regard.

Elohim! Though sorrow fill me to the brim,
Let me carefully bear the cup of myself to Thee.

Generations

for my daughter

Loving another, yet she married my father.
That other portrait faded with the years.
From her album paged in musty velvet
Glimmered forth his paling, yellowing smile.

To watch her embroider a towel or tablecloth:
She pricked the vivid silk with her nostalgia.
The stitches flowed like narrow streams of blood.
The seams were silvered with her silent tears.

And my grandmother – how little I knew of her life! –
Only her hands' tremor, and the blue seam of her lips.
How can I imagine my grandfather's love of her?
I must will myself to believe in her suffering.

No letter remains, no, not a scrap of paper
Did she leave us; only old pots in the attic
Crudely patched: tangible maimed witnesses
To a dead life: the young widow, the mother of five.

So she planted a luxuriant garden
That would embrace the newly barren house
And her new barrenness. So the trees grew,
Obedient to her will, in perfect rows.

Now my daughter is just sixteen
As I was on that quiet day in May
When I became pregnant of a single word
Scented with lilac, the remote song of a bird.

A few letters, and what is called, "a slender volume":
These are the relicts of my life. I lacked perspective
On happiness, so I ran ever faster
To escape the happy boundaries of my fate.

Listen, my daughter, never go in pursuit!
It all lies *there*, in the woven strands of blood.
How the straight trees whisper in my grandmother's garden!
Only listen! These dim echoes in my poem . . .

But what can sixteen years conceive of sorrow?
And pensiveness? the tremor of old lives?
For her, only the eternal beginnings.

Where she goes, old shadows kiss her footprints.
Somewhere, in white lilac, the nightingale
Gasps out his fragile song

Which ends always with the note of eternal beginning.

III

Pakistan

CAROLYN KIZER'S JOURNAL,

AND POEMS BY FAIZ AHMED FAIZ,

N. M. RASHID, AND M. SAFDAR MIR

Pakistan Journal

FRIDAY, SEPTEMBER 12, 1969; IN FLIGHT

As we leave Lebanon behind us, to span the mountains and oceans of dust, and salty lake-beds, and dead cities between us and our destination, I feel excited joy at returning to Pakistan after four years. In America, particularly among those of my acquaintances who have spent time in India, these feelings are met with some incredulity. But such a reaction is rare among those who know Pakistan, and have fallen under its peculiar spell.

During the time that I lived there – from September, 1964 to April, 1965 – I thought that I was maintaining a wholly detached attitude towards the place and the people, right up till the end of my visit. Then, when I went to the Lahore Airport about six in the morning, I was startled to find a contingent of about a dozen Americans and a dozen Pakistanis who had come to see me off. Decked out in the chains with silver pendants and the wreaths of jasmine or marigolds which are customary gifts to the dear departing, I climbed on the plane. My emotions were focussed on getting home and seeing my family again. Then I looked out of the plane window and saw the struggling mass of my friends alternately waving their handkerchiefs and dabbing at their eyes, and thought, how extraordinary.

"I don't feel a thing," I said to myself. The waving continued at a more frantic pace as the plane taxied off, and suddenly there was a rush of tears to my eyes, and I was beating on the plane's window and shouting – although of course they couldn't hear me – "I'll be back! I'll be back!"

As the plane took off, and turned in a great half-circle towards the south, I sat there numb: "So I'm hooked," I thought. "I am well and truly hooked, like those old relicts of the British Raj you find teaching school in the Sind or managing hotels in Peshawar, or sitting in their rockers on the porches of cottages in the Murree Hills. They never belonged, and they never will belong, but they're stuck, and so am I." By the time you realize it's happened to you, it's too late to escape. It was unnerving then, and it still is, as I return.

LATER: With the exception of a Pakistani intellectual from London, I seem to be the only person on this chartered plane-load of delegates to a scholarly conference who has been there before. As I listen to myself answering questions from every side, I feel that I am making noises like an Old – or at least Middle-Aged – Pakistani Hand. And I lived there just long enough to know how little I knew. But, by golly, I was a Lahore-wallah, and this feels more like coming home than it would to, say, Seattle, Washington, where I spent fifteen years of my life feeling like a transient.

LAHORE, SEPTEMBER 13, 3 A.M.: It's 11 p.m., London time. The temperature is about 90°, and the humidity goes right along with it. We're sitting numbly in the – thank God – air-conditioned transit lounge, waiting for a mass clearance of immigration and customs. . . . LATER: The Intercontinental Hotel was just a hole in the ground when I left. It's opposite Faletti's, that gloomy old caravanserai surrounded by huge dark trees decked with colored lights. Louis MacNiece wrote a poem on his fortieth birthday in Faletti's, his first visit since Partition. Fortunately, I have with me the diary I kept five years ago, and I look at the poem again:

> Along and back the creamed arcade
> The tall scared Sikh had paced and paced,
> Beyond the asylum of the hotel
> The Five Rivers had run to waste
> With rivers of men's blood as well,
> While on the lawn the colored lights
> And tawdry band jollied the nights
> A little along, a little back.
>
> 'So long! Come back!' So back I came
> To find Lahore a matter of course,
> At peace, and dull . . .
> Town of the Moghuls, town of fear,
> Where is your cyclist with the spear
> Who lurked so long, who looked so back?
>
> Along and back, along and round:
> Maybe the cyclist killed the Sikh,

Maybe Jahangir in his tomb,
Though slow and dead, inspired the quick
To gems of fury, flowers of doom.
No matter: this remains Lahore,
Oxcarts and tongas, as before,
Jingling along or lumbering back.

I spent my fortieth birthday here too, and wrote my poem about it.
Now Louis is dead, and Faletti's is superseded by this monster hotel,
where I stand looking at the arcades across the way, faintly silver in
the rain and dawn, and the little colored lights that burn all night.
Lahore remains Lahore. . . .
    LATER: I rise at noon, and go down to the lobby. I woke at
nine and debated: Shall I go to Anarkali Bazaar, where the writer
Intezar Husain took me, shortly after I arrived, to show me "the real
Pakistan"? We ate fresh, chopped fruit mixed with nuts (damn, I
forget what it's called), and *ferni* (a kind of smooth custard made with
rice flour and flavored with pistachio nuts, in little, disposable pottery
bowls), outside the great Wazir Khan Mosque presiding majestically
over its slums; I took my first tonga ride, and little boys ran out of the
side streets and began beating on my legs with sticks because my skirt
exposed my legs from the knees down. We went to the Pak Tea
House, where the writers hang out all day and half the night, getting
as high as talkers in an Irish pub, on coffee and the Kashmir dispute.
    Or shall I take a taxi to the Bad Shahi Mosque, my favorite struc-
ture in the world – it, and the Lahore Fort, and Jahangir's tomb, two
miles out of town, make the Taj Mahal look carved out of Ivory Soap,
to my taste. Then I could salaam in the direction of Iqbals' tomb, to
the left of the entrance. After all, today is the twenty-first anniver-
sary of the death of Mohammad Ali Jinnah, and one should pay at
least token obeisance to the poet who invented "Pakistan" for him.
    First, though, a quick swim. Five years ago I didn't see a swimming
pool in all Pakistan, though perhaps there were some tucked away in
back yards in some of the fancier establishments in Gulberg. One step
onto my balcony kills that idea. The air is as wet as the pool. I picked
up the *Pakistan Times* which had been shoved under the door. O
blessed oblivion, conferred by a highly selective memory! I had for-
gotten the true quality of that gruesome journal, where English syn-
tax has suffered such fatty degeneration that you can read the same

paragraph four times over and not have the least idea what it is trying to convey. I read the headlines with one eye shut, breaking myself in gently: FLU EPIDEMIC RAGES IN LAHORE. With a shudder, I read the weather report. I went back to bed. Now it is raining, raining, raining, great horizontal sweeps and curves across the entire sky. The scholars are milling around the lobby waiting to have their passports returned to them. Strange how many Americans, particularly inexperienced travelers like most of these, suffer from passport panic. The man in charge on arrival practically had to pry their fingers loose from their little blue-grey security symbols.

Easily I've slipped back into the old, patient rhythms. We may be here half the day. I gaze placidly out of the French doors towards the new swimming pool, cracked and empty except for rain and leaves; and an embryonic golf course stretches back to a mud village, not fifty yards from the hotel. A mud village just like the one beside my old house on Sikandar Road (named for Alexander the Great, no doubt), where the tinny, amplified voice of the mullah calling the faithful to prayer used to punctuate my days. Now, I am told, the live mullah in his minar has been replaced by a recording. "The Progress of Reaction" might be a pretty good title for a piece on the Muslim world.

Now a hotel functionary is dealing out the passports like a quick game of poker. No one knows enough to be in the least grateful for the favor done them: On my arrival, last time, I waited interminably at the pleasure of the Lahore fuzz. I remember the sight of great, rust-colored splashes on the walls of the stairway leading to Police Headquarters, shuddering at the thought they might be bloodstains of prisoners being dragged to and from interrogation. They were, of course, the stains made from spitting out chewed betel nut.

EVENING, ISLAMABAD: The rain had much abated by the time we took plane for Rawalpindi. So all that I saw of my lovely old Lahore was the great stretch of the Upper Mall lined with massive plane trees. Lahore looked fresh and clean, whether because the rains had laid her habitual red-brown dust and swept clear her avenues, or because the city has tidied itself up in recent times. I missed the camels, scooters, mendicants, holy men dabbled with dust and chalk and kohl stretched out beside the road, the cricket swarms of children, the gaudy, dilapidated tongas, the saggy taxis, donkeys, bicycles laden with tottering towers of fodder or boards, the burquas of the women providing black accents to a dusty scene. I had seen a sign announcing that the zoo is being remodeled at the cost of a couple of lakhs of rupees. Having seen the poor people of Lahore, I never had the courage to visit the zoo. . . .

The skies were clear over 'Pindi airport, which also serves Islamabad, the brand new capital. The bus drove through an ugly part of 'Pindi unfamiliar to me. I think of it as a gracious town with broad avenues, trees that rustle incessantly in the slight wind, and at night the soft – yes, soft – cawing of crows among the leaves. (Against this, the nightmare in broad day of a human spider scuttling across the avenue, ubiquitous figure out of Kafka – undoubtedly kidnapped as a child, its limbs broken and forced into this black parable of man become insect.)

From the sky, Islamabad looks as geometrical as a chessboard, defying the undulating Rawalpindi landscape, which resembles Urdu script. Approaching by car, Islamabad is indeed square, but our hotel is set apart in lots of green space, with the breathtaking Margala foothills as a backdrop.

Hundreds of cups of tea are lined up in rows awaiting us, as we fall gratefully through the door into the air-conditioned lobby. I've been thirsting for Pakistani *chai* for four long years. After several gulps of non-ambrosial liquid, I notice the tell-tale cardboard squares hanging over the sides of the pot. Lipton's, by God! And I curse as I formulate Kizer's Law of Emerging Nations: when air-conditioning comes in the window (which is promptly sealed forever), an old amenity flies out the door. When I return, five years hence, *Insha'allah*, the buses will be air-conditioned and we will be served Diet Pepsi.

Before I retire to my room, after the usual, interminable wait, I am introduced to Ralph Russell, the distinguished Urdu and Persian scholar from London University. He is small and prematurely white-haired, and full of ebullient charm. His eyes are bright as a bird's, and he talks entrancingly of Ghalib. I feel slightly better about having muffed all my chances to meet Arthur Waley. . . .

SEPTEMBER 14: My old friend, B., has arrived, and we have a beer and a chat in the late morning. I have many questions to ask him, based on a close reading of the English-language papers. I can't ask most Pakistanis, because they simply tell me that the English-language press is no good, and I should read the Urdu papers.

Yes, well I know *that*, but I don't know Urdu. I mention the increased frankness of the press since Ayub Khan's regime, citing an article on the two dozen families who control the Pakistan economy, for example. B. says he is worried about the polarization between the students, the intellectual and professional classes, and much of the working class on one side, and the *ulema* (right-wing religious leaders) on the other, backed by much of the illiterate peasantry. These religious fanatics are more dangerous, in the long run, than the wealthy and privileged, who may even have a fragmentary idea or two about social progress inasmuch as it relates to their self-interest and survival. But the *ulema* and their supporters want to drag Pakistan even farther back into a distant and partly imaginary past: total theocracy is their aim and game – all power to the pulpit! There are disturbing indications that some of the more progressive politicians, who know better, are paying increased lip-service to this, to garner votes for next year's elections.

Ayub Khan, when he took over Pakistan, was a tough military man, and considered incorruptible at that time. Like General Eisenhower, he had the approval of most of his people, and his spiritual life concerned him about as much as it did Eisenhower. However, Billy Graham is about the worst we have to offer in the way of organized hypocrisy, relatively harmless by comparison to the political ambitions of the *ulema*, who are determined to own and operate the state. Ayub continually catered to the official Islamic pieties, thereby encouraging the recrudescence of religious fanaticism. Although in a strong position, at the beginning, to bring about reform along the lines of Kemal Ataturk, curtailing the power of the *ulema*, and doing away with purdah and the veil (he might well have been less abrupt than Ataturk, and, like the present leaders of Afghanistan and Iran, liberated the young girls from the portable jail of the burqua, while allowing the older women – like old prison lags who can't endure the reality of freedom – peaceably to wear their shrouds into the grave), Ayub did very little. The tragedy of Islam: Fanaticism, all too prone to break through the membrane of gentleness, natural courtesy and spontaneous friendliness of this people, has been encouraged rather than otherwise. And it is entirely possible that our children, or the children of our children, will die horribly because of this single fact. One of every five members of the human race is a Muslim.

SEPTEMBER 15: Although the newspapers no longer re-
semble government press handouts, I notice an ominous pattern in
the headlines now: constant references to "anti-Islamic activities."
This must make some of my liberal Pakistani friends shudder all over,
the way it would affect anybody who lived in the America of the
fifties. On the lighter side, one article quotes from a booklet called,
"The Islamic Constitution," published by the Khatib of a Lahore
mosque and signed by ten *ulema*; I am particularly infatuated by
their proposed Article II: "No films will be shown in cinema houses
except those which have an all-male caste [sic]." They also advocate
the abolition of banks and insurance companies (they must own stock
in a mattress monopoly), and the reinstitution of slavery. They want
an unpaid army which will live off booty, and "each soldier will
acquire the property of the enemy whom he kills in battle." (How
would they arrange this with India and Afghanistan? Through the
U.N.?) This is a nut group; but history has taught us not to disregard
nut groups, or we may find ourselves laughing all the way to the
morgue.

SEPTEMBER 16: Yesterday, everyone went off to Taxila,
but I preferred to stay here and talk to various Pakistanis. It stormed
violently all morning, and I congratulated myself on not squelching
through the glutinous red mud of that impressive memorial to Ghan-
daran civilization. My most vivid memory of an earlier visit is pe-
ripheral to the site itself: we were invited to tea by a farm family
living in a tiny cluster of mud huts on the edge of the ruins. We sat on
a *charpoi* while my friend Tony practiced his tea-table Urdu. When
asked if I wanted milk in my *chai*, I nodded (sideways, in Urdu), and
the man of the house took my filled tea-cup into the yard and held it
under a water buffalo. Squirt! The rich milk poured from udder to
cup while a baby buffalo looked on with a certain amount of resent-
ment. That is my favorite cup of tea for all time. Sanitary too, unless
the buffalo had tuberculosis (a disease that, I am told, has now been
brought almost entirely under control).
LATER: I have been writing through most of the night, and
now, at five, I hear the ringing of bells, and the discreet taps of the
bearers on my neighbors' doors, rousing the group for an early
morning flight to Peshawar (where I am going next week, so again I

abstain). It is raining again, with furious lightning bursts, as it was when I first took plane for Peshawar five years ago, the skies black at midday. I hadn't been well all day. My only intestinal ailment in Pakistan occurred after staying at the A.I.D. Staff House in 'Pindi, which was sterilized till it squeaked, thus illustrating another of Kizer's Laws of Emerging Nations: Eat everything in moderation, so that the local bacteria don't feel rejected and wreak their revenge. It was a terribly rough flight; finally I sidled off the plane in the bitter darkness, and crouched beside a fence, where I vomited onto the tarmac. Then I threw back my head, mouth open into the strong black rain which cleansed me. I nipped back onto the plane, made up hastily, and exited ceremonially right into the arms of my reception committee, which had just pulled up. I spent that evening lying in front of a hospitable fire while various people recited poetry in Pushto, and the Head of the English Department at Peshawar (who was also a Head in current usage) smiled opaquely and gently crossed his eyes. . . .

SEPTEMBER 17: Ralph Russell made a sign in Urdu for me to prop on my typewriter. I asked him to write, "Do not touch the papers," but Ralph said that would be baffling in Urdu. After some thought, he wrote, "Do not move the papers from one place to another." Through this I have acquired great prestige with all the bearers on the floor, who believe that I wrote it. I have no intention of disabusing them unless trapped.

I show Ralph a sample sentence from a "Teach Yourself Urdu" book that I had picked up in the lobby: "The British have the biggest navel in the world." "Now I know the basis for that British air of superiority," I tell him.

I spent the better part of yesterday in 'Pindi with B. We told our driver that we wanted to get some Urdu books (recent poetry, fiction) so, quite sensibly, he took us to the Urdu textbook bazaar, a long, long, book-lined alley in the old part of the city. Neither B. nor I have been in the 'Pindi bazaars before, although he comes here on business at least twice a month. I love so much these crowded alleys, the streets of silk, the streets of brass and copper, streets for glass bangles, and bedspreads, and children's toys, and tea in bulk, and persimmons, and tailors (though I have to avert my eyes in the meat street, I confess) — the whole desperate, vivid, earth-clawing life of

the very poor – that I utterly fail to comprehend the overheard re-
marks of some scholarly delegates: "*Don't* waste your time at the
bazaar here. There's nothing to buy, and it's dirty, and smelly and
awful. . . . ."
    Our driver gamely tries again, and we find ourselves in the techni-
cal book bazaar. (To the driver, I suspect, as with the majority of
Pakistan, literature is not something written down, but something
you have in your *head* – the tales of the storytellers in the bazaars,
the hundreds of lines of Persian and Urdu poetry that thousands and
thousands of illiterate people have by heart, the songs one hears on
the street and in the tea and coffee houses – no religious prejudice in
music: Ragas are much beloved – popular music which may be set to
lyrics composed by the greatest poets living and dead: as if we had
Crashaw and Keats and Yeats and Berryman pouring out of our juke-
boxes and Muzak.)
    We ask the driver to take us downtown, and from there we walk to
a wonderful bookshop next to Shezan's restaurant, owned by a local
poet. B. buys a copy of a magazine run by the Maudoodi crowd
(Maulana Abul Aala Maudoodi, head of Jamaat-i-Islam, a right-wing
group of religious reactionaries), widely believed to be supported by
the C.I.A. B. says to the intelligent bookstore owner, "They talk too
much about Islam." "Doesn't everybody?" I remark automatically,
and raise a general laugh that I hadn't expected.
    We go to Shezan's for tea. At once we are encumbered with wait-
ers, who take our order promptly and disappear for half an hour. B.
finally collars the manager. As usual, B., a brave, wise, amusing
man, makes unpleasant truths palatable. He asks the manager to join
him in prayer. The bewildered manager asks why. "*Tea*, for the love
of Allah!" He points out that I have waited four years for a decent cup
of tea, and asks if the manager is trying for five. We are then over-
whelmed by a flurry of service. I have not only tea but pomegranate
juice, lavender and lovely. Surely if there is a paradisal liquid, it is
here, it is here, it is here.

SEPTEMBER 18: A marvelous expedition to the Murree
Hills yesterday: up, up through the mountains, on our right shad-
owy stands of giant pine, and rock outcropping that convinced one
that God is a Japanese gardener; on the left, saffron-colored valleys
surrounded by terraced slopes. Lots of corn growing. Lots of melons.

What great vineyards could be here! A girl in a flame-red *kurta* and dark green trousers stands by the door of an orange barn in the middle distance, the glowing fields at her back. I think again, resentfully, how this country has needed great artists, and how great artists need *her*. (Who can paint Rome, or the bridge at Avignon, again?) But with the old Muslim proscription against anything but decorative design, and the modern prohibitive duty on art materials of all kinds, the artists of Pakistan are either mediocre representationalists of tourist-shop quality (unless they live in Paris) or Abstract Expressionist (as they would have it) daubers, who've not had the opportunity of seeing the stream of great world painting except through the most inferior of reproductions. Yet the light, the landscape, the dramatic power of the isolated human figure, cry out for a Manet or a Corot. The trouble is – I think I'm about to promulgate another of Kizer's Laws – if an Emerging Nation happens to skip a few centuries in the rush to modernize, it can't go back and pick them up later on.

The higher we climb, the more prosperous the people. And the desperate poignancy of the children's faces down below – great glittering black eyes above the thin triangles of their cheeks – is here plumped out by cleanliness, fresh air and adequate food; the latent beauty of the Muslim people flowers, far above the hell-heat of the lowlands, where the uncounted millions of the sub-continent wear out their lives.

The first stop is Lawrence College. The Principal and all his staff are on hand to greet us, dressed in academic robes. We are ushered into the great hall for the Principal's welcoming address, in English so poor that one wonders how it can be the medium of instruction here. (But he is a lava flow of eloquence compared to his staff, who fail to understand our simplest queries.) I pass the time by reading wall plaques. One of them lists the principals since the school's founding, in 1890, as a home for British orphans whose fathers died serving the army of occupation. The first principal was the Reverend H. W. Tabernacle. And so goes the parade of English divines, M.A. Ox., until 1958 when, in larger letters and in brighter gold appears the name, Muinuddin, B.A. Dip. Ed. The school was co-educational until Partition, when of course the first move was to throw out the girls and install them in some outbuildings down the road.

The archaic British syllabus, inculcating vast amounts of irrelevant rubbish by rote (which presumably prepared little boys for future military service, and little girls to be housemaids and seamstresses) is still in force. The Principal speaks wistfully of the time when the switch to instruction in Urdu can take place.

Outside there is a huge memorial to dead graduates who took part in the Pakistan-Bharat War of 1965: three names. The one Indian member of our group, a sour soul at best, passes by it, muttering.

I try to sit through some demonstration classes, but the spectacle of these bright-eyed little boys being yoked like the buffalo to an endless treadmill is more than I can bear. I escape to the sunlight, and spot a chapel at the top of the hill. I ask the Principal about it. The dear man is under the impression that it had been a Roman-Catholic cathedral. It is locked and bolted. He asks solicitously if I would like to have it unlocked so that I might go in and pray. I say yes. So I am admitted to the Chapel of the Holy Innocents, long abandoned to the dust. It's evident that at some point the chancery was closed off from the pews, and used for instructing the primary grades in the laws of living creatures. A few glass cases stand about: in one is a pickled python; in another a stuffed squirrel who starved to death, two ravens, and a parrot, none of them labeled. In another case, grandly, is a large, iridescent bird of fierce and splendid mien. He is labeled, *Mirgh-I-Zarreen*. I stare for a long time and work it out: He is the Golden Cockerel.

I climb the stairs to the choir loft. What a sight to behold! An advanced director or playwright would weep to transport the whole thing intact, back to off-off-off-off Broadway. The old oak pews are piled with hemp, great untidy loops and heaps of red-orange hemp, layered with dust, sliced with light from gothic windows. I run down and outside to find somebody to share this with, and seize on Northrop Frye, who is contemplating a Rose of Sharon bush in full bloom.

Later, we wander through the chapel, savoring, not without nostalgia mixed with pity and despair for men, the long and pointless life of the British Raj. I sound a few notes on the organ, and the ghosts wheeze faintly, "We have done those things which we ought not to have done, and there is no health in us. But Thou, O Lord, have mercy upon us, miserable offenders. . . ." I examine the Bible on the lectern, and decide to play Bible Roulette before departing. I close my eyes, flip the pages, and stab my finger right on *I Kings* VIII: "I have surely built thee an house to dwell in, a settled place for thee to abide in forever." Dr. Frye and I exchange a long look, and walk out of the chapel and down the hill, forever.

LATER: We pile on the bus for Murree, and there walk up from the Bazaar to the circular road around the summit. Once there, Kashmir, Russia, all Asia lies piled up before our eyes.

On the way down, we collapse on the grass of the kitchen garden of the British High Commissioner, and contemplate an organized fantasy of turnip beds surmounted by a single shock of corn (did Sir James Fraser plant it, perhaps?) which looks like Louis XIV, with his attendant turnips. Some shy and beautiful children approach us. I ask them about a plant that borders the turnip court. With cries of, "Muli-muli! Muli-muli!" they pull up a long, sallow dour parsnip. It looks like Malvolio, cross-garters and all. Clearly, the altitude has gone to my head.

Departing, we have nearly reached the top of a long flight of stone steps leading back to the road when I am halted by clear bird-cries. Some distance away, the littlest girl, the loveliest of them all, is running pell-mell after me, with a bunch of marigolds. I want my life to stop, right now, right here.

STILL LATER: On the bus ride back, past opalescent mountains, through smoke, dust and moonlight, I transfer the marigolds from a heap on the floor to my capacious coat pocket. Then I proceed to sit on them. Though they look hopelessly defunct, I would as lief throw them away as the plays of Shakespeare. In my room, after they drink water for an hour or so, they are quite resurrected, glorious, gold.

SEPTEMBER 19: Up until 4 a.m. with C. who arrived last night, in time for dinner. One of the most emotional and devastating evenings I can remember. After four years during which we haven't seen each other, or even kept track of each other since the Indo-Pakistan War, nothing has changed with him. It's a passion rather like that of a medieval troubadour for a woman briefly glimpsed and fantasized about forever. But we must begin by replaying every syllable, every gesture we can recall of that time four and five years back. And *his* memory is fanatical, precise and complete, as only the inheritor of 4,000 years of oral poetry could possess. Then we must play every musical note of our separation. . . . In one way, all this is manna to my woman's ravenous heart; in another way I realize that to him I'm not anyone that I might even imperfectly recognize – almost wholly symbolic. Intently as he listens, he doesn't really listen. And what does he see?

His words flow endlessly; he cocks his head as I reply. But it is the motion of his own feelings which prompts his responses. Perhaps the suppleness of the Urdu tongue lends itself to the diminution of the distinction between language and emotion.

My marigolds, a little middle-aged, are the symbols of eternal life. I am both ruined and restored.

LATER: The conference opens officially tomorrow, and today the Pakistani delegates are streaming in – poets from Lahore and Karachi and 'Pindi, journalists who are literary men, and literary men who have abdicated in favor of journalism (although like literary men everywhere, they don't admit it), teachers from everywhere. For political reasons, East Pakistanis have absented themselves, leaving dangerous holes in the agenda.* Frantic attempts are made to patch it up. Here is D., once a poet, from Lahore, dramatically attired in native dress, with a huge Kashmir shawl thrown across his shoulder like Julius Caesar. He recoils violently when I start to hug him. It had slipped my mind that his anti-Americanism, never feeble, had come to a boil and stayed there at the time of the war with India, when he finally abjured poetry for polemic. Unlike E., a far finer poet, who is just as outspoken in his Communism, he is a rancorous man, although trimming his sails in public, except for oblique remarks in his column which often pass unnoticed, owing to the opacity of his style in English. E. on the other hand, manages to be amiable, in a detached way, to everyone, while maintaining a far tougher position. And then, being a genius, he has really transcended ideology (although for various reasons he doesn't care to say so, particularly to avoid confusing the uneducated, whose tutor he is).

D. is the only Pakistani who cold-shoulders me. I am moved by the warmth by which I am greeted and embraced by old acquaintances. The great poet, Faiz Ahmad Faiz, gives me a cordial squeeze, and spirits me off to the bar. My friend Margaret Harbottle from Peshawar, who

* I did not realize that the troubles which led to the hideous war between East and West Pakistan, which led to the founding of Bangla Desh, were coming to the crisis.

combines the finest qualities of Margaret Rutherford and Jane Aus-
ten, is here – alas, with bad news about ailing friends on the Frontier,
who are in political hot water as usual, although much of the old fuss
about the Pathan separatist movement seems to have calmed down; I
would suppose that the customary bravery of the Pathans during the
outbreak with India has had a lot to do with it.

Margaret is so great an example of what the British could have
been to India that she ought to be permanently preserved after death,
like Lenin. The British should have some kind of memento of their
presence on this great sub-continent for a hundred years. Why not,
"Margaret Harbottle Was Here"? Although she is one who became
hooked on the Northwest Provinces, she is no wan relict of the past.
She is a vigorous teacher, revered by the Pathans, despite race, sex
and national origin. I envy her that. And in her cottage garden in
Peshawar, with its ethereal, almost inhuman cranes stalking about,
and the cats purring within, she is at home.

SEPTEMBER 20: Last night I had a long fantasy about
becoming C.'s second wife (in addition to – not by elimination of –
the first Mrs. C., who is as nice as can be). The fact that I could
consider such a thing, and without jealous pangs about the present
incumbent or other ladies visible or invisible, makes me realize what
a long way I have come – a long way towards sympathizing with
certain attitudes fundamental to this society. I never thought I'd make
it. (Also, a good man is hard to find.)

LATER: The conference opened officially this morning,
with a brilliant address by Northrop Frye. He spoke of the unexpected
and astonishing rebirth of the oral tradition in modern Western lit-
erature, and how it has invalidated some aspects of the old New
Criticism. The speech was a superb bridge between the preoccupa-
tions of the Eastern and Western literary worlds represented here:
"All change takes the form of the recovery of some neglected aspect of
tradition." "Myths are culturally rooted, while folk tales are no-
madic." "Where myth exists, a magic circle is drawn around society."
"Literature is born of a specific culture and a specific locale." Each one
of these themes would serve for meditation on the present and future
direction of Asian literature. One of the major problems for the Asian
writer is how to remain within the stream of his ancient literary
traditions without becoming swamped. Another is how to deal with

the ancient carapaces of literary form. I suspect that the way you come to terms with your literary tradition is *not* to accept it in its nineteenth-century manifestations, but to tackle it deeper down and further back, and not get stuck along the way in some mode of literary antiquarianism.

As to traditional forms, such as the Urdu *ghazal* (a subject which Ralph Russell discussed in dazzling fashion), the older poets tend to keep to the form but have cracked the shell of traditional content: roses, nightingales, the Beloved, etc. – although unrequited love will always be an important strand of poetry in a society which officially disbelieves in personal love, and does a great deal to repress and punish it. So the *ghazal* may last another lifetime, or longer, but it is clear that the fragmenting of old forms is taking place here as it is everywhere else.

SEPTEMBER 21: The conference has been invited to use the swimming pool of the Islamabad Club, a mile or so from the hotel. It is patronized for the most part by families of the diplomatic missions here in the new capital. It's the finest swimming pool I have ever seen. Someone has said that it is metaphorically possible (and physically too, for that matter) in many parts of Asia to span the centuries in the course of a short walk. I think of this daily, as I walk from our modern hotel to this luxurious pool, through a landscape and past a people unchanged for a thousand years. Encapsulated culture-shock produces a pervasive sense of unreality: Someone at the pool remarks casually, "I see a unicorn over there." Ah yes, a unicorn. I look up, quite unsurprised. There is a man dressed like a Brigadier.

Listening to the idle talk around the pool, I am amused by the way many of the scholars generalize about the culture here, on the flimsiest evidence. How indignantly they would review a book based on such superficial research and such subjective reactions! Yet here they are, wrapping up a whole society in a catch-phrase or two.

I attract a certain amount of attention because I wear twenty-four glass bangles in swimming. (Too much trouble to take them off. Anyhow, you have to be a little drunk in order to make your hand flexible as a porpoise. Otherwise the bangle snaps, and you sustain a nasty cut in the fleshy part of the thumb.) Bangles. . . . I remember when Miss Altaf Fatima, the short, pudgy, heroic novelist (who lived next to the movie theatre, where the multiple-features accompanied her thoughts most of the night), in the cheapest of cotton saris, took me to Anarkali to buy me bangles. They cost only a few annas apiece. Another Welcome to Pakistan gesture. Bangles, the People's Jewelry. *Nobody* is too poor to wear bangles. Bangles, like the poor, have lives that are brief and fragile, and like the poor they are expendable. Bangle Time: day by day by day, they snap, and fall away, leaving your arm naked again: existential time. Bangles bestowing grace: my arm dips in the water as I swim and lifts in a graceful arc – all because of bangles glinting in the light, shedding a thousand drops of water in crystal cascades. It is well known that in a sari (or even a burqua, God forfend!) your walk becomes undulant and sexy. Add a lot of tinkling jewelry to the rustle of silk. Easy. More difficult: add a head of long, oiled, perfumed silken hair that falls down your spine to the back of your knees in a braided coil as thick as your arm. Grace incarnate. (Sour postscript: Then waste 98% of your femininity in the company of other women, mainly relatives, where almost the sole topic of conversation is where you obtained your finery and how much it cost – while the men are off having what they think is a good time. I love to recall the remark made by a woman friend of mine in – I am happy to say – the American diplomatic service, at a typical party consisting of around forty men and the two of us. Fed up at last, she said, "When I first came to this country I was sorry for the women. Now I'm sorry for *you*. You don't know what you're missing.")

I bought the bangles in the Murree bazaar. For so long I've been yearning for bangles and *pan* – the collection of mild narcotics bound up in betel leaf and folded like a diaper. Two bangles broken so far. (The bangle-wallah had given me two baker's dozen.) My aging marigolds, still bright, and my bright bangles: Eternity versus existential time.

LATER: I went with B. and his wife, just arrived, to a reception in 'Pindi given by the Minister of Education and a clutch of Cabinet members and big shots, and their good ladies. The B's are living proof that even this system can produce a happy marriage. Although I persist in believing that there are more actively unhappy marriages here than in the West – or perhaps it would be more accurate to say more marriages where, in the words of my friend, they don't know what they're missing.

At the reception, with that old-time hypocrisy which irritates me so intensely, they served only orange drink and the local cola. If all the men didn't drink their heads off in the privacy of their own homes, as the phrase has it, I wouldn't mind so much. As it is, it's like the Catholic Church trying to ban contraception for the rest of us. Or perhaps they just don't want to suffer watching us drink while they abstain. I was annoyed enough to lead a rump group into the hotel bar, after checking with a couple of Pakistani pals to see if that would constitute Impossible Behaviour. Not at all, they said wistfully.

I came back to the dining-room just in time for Faiz to lead me over to a table where it was wall-to-wall poets, including D., who proceeded to make rude remarks about me in Urdu. I was tempted to regale the group with stories about how he used to show up at my house in Lahore at all hours, in his Pakistani drag, go through a series of ritual courtship motions much like those of a trumpeter swan, and then sit back and wait for me to drop dead from joy. After I left Pakistan he gave up, and married his mother, or somebody. Now I restrained myself, in memory of his early, lovely poems.

I spent most of the evening being told stories by Faiz, an enchanting talker, both at dinner and back at the bar later on. I remember the first time I saw Faiz, sitting quietly on the platform at a *mushira* (a large, group outdoor poetry-reading, under a canopy) waiting his turn to read. Even before he spoke – and of course I couldn't understand when he did – I knew without hesitation that he was a great man. How?

SEPTEMBER 22: For days the letters column of the paper has been taken up with a subject both ominous and encouraging: ominous that it happened, encouraging that people are making a fuss, and that the paper prints their letters. When I was here before, probably the ablest Pakistani professor of English in the country was Eric Cyprian of Islamia College. He required, and produced, a high standard of English prose and poetry. Recently he was abruptly discharged from his post for, 1) anti-Islamic activities, and 2) lack of funds to pay his salary. He was within months of retiring with a pension. Now he doesn't even get severance pay. He will be utterly destitute, as the salary scale for professors permits them to accumulate nothing but debts.

The letter-writer's standard line of defense of Professor Cyprian probably wouldn't make a good impression on either the A.C.L.U. or the A. A. U. P. A sample, under the running head, "A Sordid Affair" (I should say that the word "sordid" seems very popular among Pakistani intellectuals and journalists): "Sir, Every pupil of Mr. Cyprian must have been shocked to hear of his dismissal . . . I beg to cite just one incident: It was the month of Ramazan. We were having a meeting of The Young Writers. One young man lit a cigarette. Nobody took any notice of him except Mr. Cyprian. He made the smoker put out his cigarette, saying, 'You must respect the month of Ramazan.' As for the second objection, I say that no salary is too high for a kind, devoted and sincere teacher like Mr. Cyprian. Yours, etc."

I used to visit Cyprian's classes, to talk about American poetry, and to read the students' work and comment on it. The subject matter of much of their writing was obsessed with the cataclysm of blood, fire and brimstone, which was their earliest memory: Partition. This was a time when, at two or three years old, you were dug from the bottom layer of bodies by frantic hands, barely breathing, often wounded yourself, in a railway car in Lahore station, where every adult in that car had been slaughtered. Your parents had flung themselves protectively on you, in their last moments. If they died without being disemboweled or mutilated in ways too horrible to mention, by the Sikhs of Shrinigar, as the train passed through the station, they were the fortunate dead. Can this be written of in the stately couplets and intricate rhymes of the *ghazal*?

But, not long before my stay in Pakistan, Allen Ginsberg had penetrated the sub-continent. (This is an over-simplification, but even so, the tremendous *positive* impact of his visit, in contrast to the scandalous impact which most people know about vaguely, can hardly be overestimated.) Through the influence of Ginsberg and his large and immediate following, free verse did more than liberate form; it liberated consciousness. Through it, the students discovered the instrument of their catharsis.

When asked to "criticize" such work, Cyprian and I tended to throw up our hands. How do you criticize a volcanic eruption? Never mind. As we have seen with our own writers who happen to be black, the shouts of pain and rage, or grievance and horror, precede the ability to create a controlled work of art. Liberation now, literature later.

But it is precisely at this point, when young writers need to make new accommodations between their traditions and their immediate experience (post-catharsis), that the help of teachers like Eric Cyprian is urgently required if they are to become artists, or even self-comprehending men and women. That is why I am so gloomy that he – and no doubt others like him – has been driven from his post. And I, as an American, am in absolutely no position to do anything to help. I confirm this with B. later, who says to stay out of it. I: "What about money?" B. (severely): "We will see that he is cared for." Bless B. I'd like to give many examples of his goodness and courage, but they would identify him too clearly, in these uncertain times.

SEPTEMBER 23, 6 A.M.: I am to give my paper this morning, and then depart at once for Peshawar by car, to catch up with a party of people going to Swat, then to Afghanistan and Iran. I've always wanted to go to Swat, "because of Babe Ruth," I tell my Pakistani friends. Even if I explained it, I wouldn't explain anything. But that helps make up for all the jokes in Urdu that I don't get.

Yesterday, various emissaries from the group going to Swat came by this hotel to look for me. Everyone to whom they spoke, from manager to busboy, assured them that I was in conference, they didn't know where, and could under no circumstances be disturbed even if they did know. The hotel people were perfectly aware that I was in the bar with Faiz all afternoon, drinking gin and going over translations. They damned well weren't going to interrupt us. They know how to treat poets in this country.

SAIDU-SHARIF, SWAT, 8 P.M.: My speech went over reasonably well. I closed by reading a poem of Faiz. He graciously came forward and recited it in Urdu before I read my English version. We brought down the house with that, although I could see some Pakistanis looking peevish at the translation – it is a *very* famous poem. But for the most part they were the kind who believe that you can't translate *anything* without losing *everything*; and people of this sort are the principal reason why the bulk of Urdu literature is so little known in the West. As I used to say to my Pakistani friends when I lived here, "Would you rather have a door open a crack into a beautiful garden, or would you prefer to keep it locked and bolted?"

Here is the poem, much improved by yesterday's session in the bar:

IF I WERE CERTAIN

If I were certain, o my dear companion,
If I were certain that your muffled pulse,
Grief in your eyes, heart in your breast afire
Could be relieved by my devoted care,
If sympathetic phrases were a cure
To lift the sterile shadows from your brain,
To wipe the stain of insult from your brow,
And to restore your failing youth again;
If I were certain, o my dear companion,
I would nurse you day and night without repose.
How I would croon you tender, moving songs,
Tunes of cascades, of spring, and orchard blossoms,
Morning's commencement, the traveling moon and planets,
How I would spin you long, romantic tales!
Tales of proud girls whose stiff, unyielding bodies
Melt beneath the urgent warmth of hands,
How the features, learned by heart, of a single face,
Alter at once, and bloom before your eyes,
How the marmoreal pallor of her skin
Warms, of a sudden, with a glow like wine.
How roses bend meek stems that you may pluck them,
And how the imperial night bursts into fragrance.
Then I would sing, sing endlessly for you,
Weaving my songs, kneel endlessly beside you.
No song of mine can be a panacea
For suffering, though it may soothe your grief.
My song is not a lancet but a salve
Anointing the long anguish of your life.
Only a knife can end your agony,
Killing, redeeming. I cannot fulfill you
Nor any breathing being on this earth
Except yourself, except yourself, except yourself.
                                        —*Faiz Ahmad Faiz*

SEPTEMBER 24: I split for Swat, right on schedule – good
to make a fast getaway, and avoid prolonged and painful farewells.
The driver made fine time out of Islamabad, and soon we swung onto
The Grand Trunk Road. The world's greatest road. The road between

Europe and Asia, between India and Greece, the route of Alexander, Tamurlaine and Genghis Khan, the road built by the greatest man of all, to my mind, the first Moghul Emperor, Akbar, who created more than he destroyed, who created much that still lives today. Road of traders, and armies, and nomads and fierce tribesmen, and bandits, of thousands upon thousands of caravans, camels, donkeys, horsemen, and peasants transporting their produce or fleeing their oppressors, measuring off the miles with two bare feet – road mercifully and blessedly unchanged.

As the driver tore along, I hung my head out of the car window, singing over and over, "Oh the Grand Trunk Road is a grand trunk road," exhilarated as all hell, and mad to see everything once more. At the same time I was holding back tears at having to leave my friends, and C. For another half a decade, I suppose. Well, never mind. Age cannot wither me in those eyes. And custom is damned well not going to stale my infinite variety, worse luck.

I held myself in suspense, not wanting to miss the first glimpse of a place I love: Attock Fort, at the confluence of the great Kabul and Indus Rivers. First, a couple of small, ruined caravanserais (built by Akbar, I bet); then the graveyard, and a bare, ruined mosque; then around the curve, and Attock Fort! Built by Akbar, its massive walls swoop down the hills to the river in waves of scalloped stone. (I have about eighty-five photographs of it at home, none of them any good.) Then we go down past the village which separates the fort from the road, to the famous suspension bridge built by the British. After the bridge, the road wanders along the river for a while, then gives itself a shake and takes off in a straight line, on a dead run, for the Frontier. At Nowshera, an old army town just this side of Peshawar, I see some soldiers making the only sensible use that I can imagine of a couple of armored tanks: grading a road. Let us beat our tanks into road-graders. . . .

We roll up to Dean's Hotel, in Peshawar, with about eleven minutes to spare.

The car broke down five times on the way to Swat, so we missed a visit to a Buddha carved in rock which has lost most of its frontage, according to my fellow-travelers. But, being tardy, we hit the Swat Valley at just the right time, late afternoon: Low sun nearing the mountains' rim, but still gleaming on green-yellow fields that give off an unearthly glow. The fields divide for a pure blue river, gliding along its broad bed. It took me quite a while to realize that the rich green crop we saw was *rice*. I'm familiar with Chinese rice fields: peasants sloshing through icy mud to harvest puny stalks no higher than your hand. This glorious stuff must be waist-high. Oceans of chartreuse rice! And melons, huge mounds of melons, like orange balloons. And nomads: stunning women, striding along with erect backs, looking you dead in the eye. (What a contrast to all that burqua-bundling and scarf-grabbing and sideways-shuffling apprehension down below!) They are dressed in a profusion of clashing prints and jangling jewels that would send Vuillard and Bonnard into fits.

The hotel is a superb old place, with ample lawns and huge trees, formerly the Wali's guest house. Our timing is not all that it might be. Today the Government put the Wali, and the heads of the other Frontier states, out of business. Their principalities are now Districts. The Wali, poor Wali, was supposed to receive us. Olly, olly, oxenfree, Wali! But the Wali is lurking, and skulking, and sulking, deep within his walls. He is weeping at the bitter ingratitude of men and states. He sends a Cabinet Minister (as of yesterday) in his place, who makes sad, polite noises to us, and we make sleepy polite noises back. And then we go tumble into our beds, by the light of a huge full moon. All goodly report of Swat is right: Paradise lives!

SEPTEMBER 25, KABUL, AFGHANISTAN: Swat left me speechless. Anyway, the less people know about the splendors of Swat, the better. The whole place ought to be Classified Information, or all sorts of unworthy types will be wanting to go there and spoil it. Wednesday a day of desultory sightseeing and mooning around. We drove back to Peshawar on Thursday. Wandered about in the bazaar for a while, everything permeated by the lovely, smoky, sandalwood-sweet odor of hashish. You can get high just walking around. An evening of "ethnic dancing" on the lawn of Dean's Hotel, the only amusing part of it the way the other western guests went into raptures about the two dancing girls, who were boys. Typical Pathan tarts they were, too, tough as nails, throwing in a bump here, a grind there, and batting their eyes at the guests in a parody of lust.

This morning we climbed on buses and headed for the Khyber Pass. When I was here before, I got myself adjudged a suspicious character in the eyes of the authorities because I spent too much time with the Pathan poets, some of whom were suspected of being involved with the Red Shirts, or Pathan separatist movement. When I wasn't avoiding a bumbling oaf from the C.I.A. (in those innocent days I thought the Pakistanis were paranoid about the C.I.A. – now, of course, I know better), for fear I might be thought a colleague or pal of his, I was trying to avoid well-meaning officials of both governments, who tried to dissuade me from staying near Charsadda Village with friends of mine, an experience I wasn't about to miss. My host was perhaps the best poet writing in Pushto; at any rate his poems were once used in school and college textbooks, before he got in too much political trouble. He is the son of the illustrious Abdul Ghaffar Khan, known as "the Gandhi of the Frontier," now an ancient man who is forced to live exiled in Kabul, but still a potent symbol to his followers and to his enemies. Why the Pakistani authorities worried about his son Ghani is more than I can understand. Years of prison (mostly under the British), drink, drugs, failing health and spiritual dishevelment would seem a more than effective bar to his leading a tribal uprising. Furthermore, no man as totally obsessed with art and poetry as Ghani has time for politics. But the story of my friendship and love for Ghani, and Roshan, his wife, is a book that I am not going to open now. All this was by way of explaining why I didn't get to the Khyber Pass in 1965. One good feint toward Afghanistan, and I probably would have been declared *persona non grata*, and pushed out of the country.

It is a fine, clear morning as we roll toward the border. The entrance to the pass is not impressive, and we are held up the usual length of time while passports are inspected. I run into the weedy son and heir of the Meer of Hunza, who was a child when I met him last in Lahore, in the hall of the Customs and Immigration Building. I suppose the poor old Meer is out of a job, too. It is amusing to introduce "the Crown Prince," wearing an ancient sweater, sneakers, and jeans, to a couple of impressionable people in our party, who barely refrain from dropping him a curtsey.

At last we're off. The mountains begin to draw closer, but I am craning my neck to stare back at the Pakistan border – a wooden gate, a cluster of shacks and parked cars, a couple of wooden conning towers and a lot of troops – for as long as I can. But I can't really see very well. I seem to be crying again. Goodbye, Pakistan! So long! I'll be back! I'll be back!

Bangla Desh : I

The festival of massacre: how make it vivid?
How entertain you with the mourning of my blood?
My emaciated body is nearly drained of blood:
Not enough to light the lamps.
Not enough to fill the goblets;
Nor to light any fires,
Nor to slake any thirst.
My lacerated body is nearly drained of blood.
But every vein brims with a fatal poison;
Every drop is the fury of a cobra,
Distilled from the anguish and pain of centuries,
Enflamed with the passionate fury of decades.
Beware of my body! It is a river of poison.

Beware of my body. It is a charred log in the wilderness.
If you attempt to burn it in your garden compound,
Instead of the jasmine and the rose,
The thorns of my bones will flower.
If you scatter my body over the hills and valleys,
Instead of the perfume of the morning breeze,
You will fling away the dust of my anguished soul.
So beware. Because my heart is thirsting for blood.

Bangla Desh : II
The Blood in My Eyes

Layer by layer, the dust of bitterness
Silts up my heart till it reaches my eyes.
There is nothing for it; I must obey my healer:
Rinse my eyes with blood.
Now my blood-filled eyes see red:
The sun that was gold is blood.
The silver moon is blood.
Each tree is a pillar of blood;
Each flower an eye dipped in blood;
Each gaze is spun on a thread of blood.
Every image is smeared with blood.

The bloodstream flows with the brilliant crimson of anger,
Of suffering, of the passion of martyrdom.
When the blood clots, turns black,
It vanishes in darkest night, in death,
Where all color strangles and drowns.
Don't let this happen, my healer!
Send me a river of tears,
The baptismal waters.
Then, bathed in that river,
Perhaps my eyes, my heavy, dust-laden eyes,
Will be cleansed of blood forever.

Bangla Desh : III
Revisited After the Holocaust, 1973

Ghazal

We who are strangers now, after our years of easy friendship;
How many times must we meet, before we are reacquainted?

How can we reclaim that old camaraderie?
When shall the eye see once more that spring of spotless green?

How many monsoons are required
To wash away the stains of blood?

Merciless, merciless was the moment when love ended.
Cruel, cruel were the mornings, after the nights of tenderness.

As heartbreak gave no respite, the heart yearned
To quarrel as friends once more, after the prayers for forgiveness.

But the word I had come here to speak,
With the offering of my life as sacrifice,

That reconciling word remained unspoken
After everything else had been said.

Elegy for Hassan Nasir

(Killed by torture in the Lahore Fort, 1959)

Today, all at once, when the thread of my vision snapped,
The sun and moon were smashed to bits in the skies.

Like my heart, no trace of the road of faith remains.
Now, where I stand, there is neither light nor dark.

Now, let someone else tend the garden of sorrow!
Because, friends, in my heart the nourishing dew has dried.

The riot of madness has subsided.
The rain of stones has ended.

And, in the path of the Beloved,
The banner of my blood has been unfurled.

The dust of the road stained red as the mouth of the Beloved;
Let me see who is willing to take my place when I am gone.

"Who else can drain the murderous wine of love?"
The cry heard again on the lips of the Saqi, when I am gone.

Izhab-O-Rasai
(Expression and Reach)

Paintbrush and lute-string or new modeling clay
Are ways of saying what we want to say.
But we, who wrote once of lovers coming together,
How can we speak, now, of the whole world's weather?
What we would reach is always out of reach.
The end of art is not the end of speech.

Within each heap of ashes gleams a spark
Of pained and random passion in the dark,
Driven without volition by the heat
Within its breast, to move on drunken, dancing feet
To where creation bursts like song, deranged,
But from itself perpetually estranged.
Yet here conjoined are colors, curves and lines:
Divinity rules the meaning it divines.

A single ray of this impulsive gleam
May whirl the months and years into a dream,
Twitching the limbs of any drowsing dancer,
To an old potter at his wheel, revealing answer:
Poetry! Fashioning the bricks without the clay,
Dark tenements suffused with deathless day.

To whom shall I address my artful speech
When you are lost, eternally out of reach?
Two lovers now become our whole estate.
But I am lost, my muse, its burdensome weight
That I long to lay down with my life, to share
With you, apathetic reader. But you don't care.

Elegy

In the May breeze
            the water-lily sways
                        on a wave of water.

In the May breeze
            my heart sways
                        on a wave of ardor.

In the May breeze
            my branch of jasmine,
                        you went to sleep

In the May breeze
            under the earth
                        just a year ago.

IV

Yugoslavia

A PROSE POEM ON TRANSLATION, AND

NINE TRANSLATIONS FROM THE MACEDONIAN

Translation

I am now utterly translated into Macedonian, after two days and nights, non-stop in Skopje. Never has anyone been so well and truly translated. I feel that I, myself, have been translated. Henceforth, I shall write *only* to be translated. All complexities have been eliminated. All polysyllables. All ambiguities. All multiple meanings. All humor. My new poetry is of such a transparency that it virtually has no identity at all. It is a glass vessel, waiting to be filled with the colorful fluid which is translation. In creation, now, the only question is, "Yes, but how will it sound in Macedonian?" I will greet you, hug you, and hand you this, on the morrow – hand you this wordlessly, because, alas, you do not speak Macedonian. Perhaps you can pick up a few words if you try, for we must have a common language, if only to hug in.

for Lars Gustafsson

Professional Poet

The last word, the last hasty swallow

you get up from the table, after your working day
and catch the first bus to the kitchen
you tear off a hunk of bread, inhale the good oven odors
Your body, leaden with weariness, the mold
you cram with rich food
Switch on the set
                        and inspect the back yard
through another screen
                                with a wet finger
you flip the pages of the sky.

Nothing will come of nothing.
                                Clematis tendrils
float in the void . . . "THEY MUST BE TRAINED ON A TRELLIS"
your daughter brings you a chair
The table is set, your wife calls
through the window of a parallel world.

After dinner, you walk in the garden
alone in your pressurized space-suit,
                        stars all around you
even beneath you. Your antennae must be redirected.
The pear tree, newly pruned, requires manure.

Back to the module:
                Daddy, what does it mean
to be a monster?
                Suddenly, the chain of command dissolves
bits of paper whirling in free fall
around the table:
                untouched paper
and your pencil, ominous as a revolver.

Flood at the International Writer's Workshop

Since the sky started crying
I haven't been out-of-doors for thirty-one days:
By now the earth must be a pair of pliers
With tatters of human flesh stuck to its jaws.

I imagine myself on a see-saw, balanced so lightly
That if even an atom fell on it (let alone a bomb)
I would be hurled like a stone from a catapult
Straight back into the trap of Macedonia.

My people, are we God's voracious eye
Suspended in the air like a traffic-light
Which, as it blinks, directs the flow of nations?
Right now I'm only that greedy eye of legend
Which, on my side of the scale, outweighs the world.

In the Ark, our elevators work erratically:
Every deck is bursting with trapped livestock!
On the first floor, insects have turned into neurons
Without any owners:
On the second, saurians form a mythic chain
To swallow each other so they will all disappear,
But too feeble to achieve total consummation;
On the third floor, the mad vegetarians
Roaring with hunger, lay waste the frigidaires;
On the fourth, the carnivorous flowers
Make plans to devour God;
On the fifth floor, this lone Macedonian
Mangles their languages, recreating Babel.

And every line that occurs to me sinks like a plummet
When it should splash about like a happy dog
And, like a dolphin, jump through its trainer's hoop.
But I'm dense when it comes to featherweight words!
The verb should be in a state of constant erection,

In equal readiness to strike, or stroke;
The adjective stick to the noun
                          like a lizard catching flies;
And the noun should swing both ways,
While the conjunctive is a universal pass-key.

So the sky sobs on, like an hysterical child,
Like the she-dragons of my legends.
The gutters gurgle, and gargle.
The drain-pipes are subterranean Mississippis.

The words refuse to swallow us any longer
Now we have set them to quarreling among themselves:
Trying to strangle each other, they bite off their tongues.
They have burned to tell us everything they know,
But, being dumb now, drooling idiots,

Speechlessly, they copulate with rainbows.

My Sister's Letter

Your letter wrecked my day.
I read and re-read it, till
                    the words blurred into gibberish.
How can I be expected to go on writing
When you refuse to explain what happens at home?
We are separated by thousands of miles of silence.
Here too, I'm imprisoned in ignorance.

I'm expected to put my ear to this alien earth
– as we used to do as children, listening
                    for the tremor of unseen trains.
Haven't you learned by now
That even the ground has learned how to dissemble?
No train arrives – only a false vibration.
The land has learned to hold its breath, play dead.

Thanks very much for your silence.
                    Now I'm utterly dismayed.
You go on spinning sentences out of emptiness . . .
                    Are you trying to be the poet
Instead of me?
Somehow I managed to survive the day.
I've had practice staying alive;
                    What choice do we have?
Deep into sleep, swamped by a sea of nightmares
A voice I thought was yours awakened me:
                    screaming, "Help! help!"
Having fallen on the bed without undressing,
I could have rushed downstairs into the lobby,
                    aroused the desk-clerk
To call the police.
                    But who would have believed me,
Phantom victim of a phantom cry?
"Help!" once again
                    and then the voice broke off . . .

Thoughtfully, I put on my pyjamas.
                    What does any of it matter?
Even the dead still cry out in their sleep,
Protest injustice, screaming from the grave
                    for vindication,
Still persecuted by the living
                    survivors who defame them,
Who conspire to pretend we are all deaf to the dead.

But at least they don't send me empty letters
So that I tremble with all they fail to say.

1. When I Came Back

When I came back
from discovering America
unfinished phrases drifted in the wind
samara for commas

and the wind tied my reed flute
into a knot.

My old clothes were returned to me
re-cut in my absence
to fit the image you had of me.

When I put them on
they split at the seams.

2. On the Way Back

London

When we speak of freedom
our breathing is as casual
as flight for birds,

when it should be hard labor
which tires us out,
so tired
that we may not show up for work.

Only this effort
not automatic, achieved by an act of will,
could give back breath to the dead.

3. Prostitution

Provocatively, our epoch swings her breasts.
Who will suck at her tits?
– Who won't?
As she passes my window, I get a whiff
of her randy scent.

At night, when I'm stretched on my back,
the whole world turns on my axis.

After a while
an old crone will come by,
slightly touched in the head,

who will try to pay me
for my favors.

Climate and Lyre

Where is the sky born?
Or will my triumph be recorded
Only in my sad eyes which face Olympus?
O my soul, the seasons change the climate
Like gamblers dealing cards.
Why do you echo in my ear
This random note of sorrow?

I don't know if my country really needs me
But I give myself to her with words
As if I were an unknown warrior.
Suddenly, color invades the void;
With a bronze resonance, a poplar leaf
Drops from its stem.

A harsh word breaks my lyre in two.
Sky, where are your lightnings?
The tree, in its grief for the bird,
Begins to resemble the bird.

from *Equinox*

This is an hour of calm, a quiet hour,
an idyll of days and nights like a folding of hands
the sky soft on the stretched body of the plain
Now is the hour when nothing happens
as if the world didn't breathe, as if the rain didn't pour
a dream enclosed in the dark of a hazelnut
a stone forgotten under the body of a hill
Now is the instant when wheat is harvested
when the chimney doesn't smoke nor the road resound
Man lies beneath the body of the sun
distilled into nothing by its shadows
This is the total moment: the balance of black and white.

from *Samuel*

(from part 1 of a 5-part dramatic poem)

There was nothing left for man:
The lava rose over the horror,
Overflowing the gulfs,
Leveled the chasms.
The rivers were effaced
By the rock,
          Hard, black rock.

The moon no longer set
Over the axis of the plains.
Grain was no longer seen on the threshing floors.
The trees bore rock instead of fruit,
And the peasants took it in their hands like bread.
And instead of children, the pregnant women
Brought forth rock:
          Hard, black rock.

The wild animals howled through the forests.
The last she-wolf died on a dry outcropping.
She will no longer give birth to wolves.

And the wide winds, driven mad,
Blew enormous ashes
And heaped them on one another,
And, higher than centuries, pushed the rock,
The bare rock, the black rock.

Nothing, nothing left for man.
It rose up over the horror,
And the gulfs overflowed,
The chasms leveled,
The rivers effaced
By the rock,
The bare rock, the black rock.

V

African Presence

A TRANSLATION FROM THE FRENCH

OF EDOUARD MAUNICK AND

A POEM BY CAROLYN KIZER

Sept Versants Sept Syllables

pour Aimé Césaire et Pierre Emmanuel

I

si tu venais de toi-même
en ce lieu contradictoire
refaire fête de l'ébène
le métal des premiers temps

> si tu essayais le rêve
> avant que d'être inutile
> avant le rebond du sang
> avant la mort de ton père

ce pays était miroir
la mer en guise de tain
les îles à suée de rames
de clefs se ceignaient les reins

> le bonheur était partout
> et nulle part à surprendre
> si tu jouais l'océan
> une dernière fois sur la terre

mais qu'est-ce la dernière fois
pour un poète sans race
son corps toujours se répète
parmi les témoins d'en face

> il suit sans les découvrir
> les chemins de la colère
> son pays est ce pays
> où tous les pays vertigent

Seven Sides and Seven Syllables

for Aimé Césaire and Pierre Emmanuel

I

happen you come on your own
to this contradicted place
re-celebrate ebony
the original metal

> happen you essay the dream
> before you outlive yourself
> before the blood surges back
> before your father expires

this land once was a mirror
which was silvered by the sea
in the sweat of oars, islands
with keys girded up their loins

> good fortune surrounded us
> in no way surprising us
> if we wager on the sea
> for the last possible time

but what can be the last time
for the deracinated?
again, those who oppose him
share the flesh of the poet

> unaware, he keeps going
> not heeding all the mad ways
> all countries merge dizzily
> in this country of his own

II

mon amour est improbable
vienne le goût de salive
le signe de neutralité
à fleur du jardin natal

> ici les roses sont roses
> défense le glaïeul
> un homme qui parle debout
> se bande les yeux de pluie

nous prenons fortes racines
à l'heure de la mise à mort
là-bas les grilles sont peintes
aux couleurs des équinoxes

> un homme qui parle debout
> s'abolit dans le symbole
> je dis rose et c'est l'espoir
> qui donc vivra de ce jeu

qui prendra le glaïeul
dans sa forme de coupe-coupe
pour nouer avec le sang
métis dans sa survivance

> je nomme jardin la terre
> la terre sans exception
> qui donc plantera les grilles
> sinon les miens sinon moi

moi cet enfant de mille races
pétri d'Europe et des Indes
taillé plus profondément
dans le cri du Mozambique

II

my love is improbable
let the saliva well up
neutrality, its token
skimming the garden of birth

> here the roses are roses
> sword-lilies prohibited
> a man who speaks standing up
> has his eyes bandaged with rain

we all take powerful root
on assassination day
with the garden's iron pickets
stained bright by the equinox

> here a man who speaks standing
> is submerged in the symbol:
> I say rose and it means hope
> but who will live by this game?

who will take up sword-lilies
in their form of machetes
to knot up with blood once more
what survives as a mongrel?

> the whole world I name garden
> I leave no place unbaptized
> who will plant garden fences
> if not I, or my kinfolk?

I, the child of all races
soul of India, Europe,
my identity branded
in the cry of Mozambique

III

> ainsi je suis anonyme
> et je garde l'héritage
> de vos triques ancestrales
> de votre fuite d'hommes noirs

je pourrais porter vos noms
sans jamais être nommé
porter votre numéro
sans jamais être compté

> commander vos places fortes
> me vêtir de votre peur
> reconnaissable du feu
> reconnaissable du vent

de ce qui bâtit l'exil
le feu le vent sur la mer
reconnaissant les racines
de l'arbre jamais reconnu

> reconnaissant les racines
> je me tais en signe de deuil
> sur la part non partagée
> je suis nègre de préférence

j'ai lu Senghor et Césaire
et Guillèn et Richard Wright
mais Saint-John Perse et Lorca
Dylan Thomas et Cadou

> et debout Paul Eluard
> réinventent la mémoire
> si tu sortais du miroir
> pour unir matin et soir

III

> thus I am anonymous
> while holding the heritage
> of your ancestral truncheons
> and your black man's evasions

I could accept your labels
and stay unidentified
be tattooed by your numbers
while remaining uncounted

> command all your battlements
> cloak myself in your panic
> recognizing the thunder
> and recognizing the wind

know the substance of exile:
on the sea, wind and thunder
recognizing all the roots
of the tree that rejects me

> recognizing all the roots
> tongue-ties me with bereavement
> on the shore of denial
> I will choose to be Negro

I've read Senghor and Césaire
and Guillèn and Richard Wright
but Lorca and St. John Perse
Dylan Thomas and Cadou

> Paul Eluard, vertical
> all reinvent memory
> you step out of the mirror
> to marry morning with night

IV

à fendre pierre l'amertume
qui me monte à la parole
au bout de tous les versets
faut-il que je sois de haine

                              un vocable appareillant
                              vers lieu de neige et de feu
                              des mots de mauvaise haleine
                              des images à brûle-peau

des désirs amers et purs
de tumultueux silences
j'épelle ici mon poème
délivrant l'amour de vous

                              ne pas dire ce qu'il faut dire
                              diviser le sang du sang
                              habiter d'autres demeures
                              que les demeures habitables

ce n'est pas facile l'exil
malgré les frontières tues
les portes claires les mains vives
ce n'est pas facile jamais

                              accepter est un refus
                              refuser une colère
                              donnez-moi vos libres livres
                              et vos christs à peine d'homme

promis j'apprendrai la chair
comme à travers l'eau des lacs
je tuerai la mer ancienne
brûlerai les cargaisons

IV

rising in me, the promise
my mouth will spit bitterness
to crack the rejecting rock
at the end of all stanzas

                utterance moves toward a place
                where snow, thunder cohabit
                of words fouled by long weeping
                of visions searing the skin

with desires pure and bitter
tumultuous silences
I here spell out my poem
releasing my love of you

                withholding what must be said
                dividing my blood from blood
                inhabiting somewhere else
                than the habitable space

exile is no easy thing
despite obscure boundaries
open doors and living hands
no, it is never easy!

                to accept is to refuse
                refusal reveals anger
                fling open your registers!
                bring your mortal crucifix!

I swear to understand flesh
transparent as lake water
I shall murder ancient seas
set fire to their slave cargoes

V

         mais CHRIST cette odeur de chaînes
         ce frottement de métal
         contre les os en défaite
         et ces quinconces de cordes

j'ai la force de mes yeux
mais c'est triste à regarder
des chiens dressés contre noirs
des cantiques poignardés

         oui regarder chavirer
         des voix de femmes et d'enfants
         dont le crime est vertical
         qui ne savent plus ramper

sont-ce là Noël et la paille
et notre poésie blanche
et notre poésie noire
toute entière notre poésie

VI

         je ne revendique pas
         tirant avec vos fusils
         guérissant avec vos mains
         j'ai froid et faim pour nous tous

s'il était un territoire
entre midi et minuit
c'est là que j'irais crier
mon sang mêlé jusqu'à l'âme

         car je vous préfère en moi
         sans couleur ni passeport
         je sais nous rêvons de Dieu
         et sommes tous pardonnés

V

> but CHRIST, this odor of chains
> and this rattling of metal
> against the defeated bones
> these quincunxes of ropes!

I can force my eyes to see
but the sight is too tragic:
dogs trained to attack the blacks
and their spirituals stabbed

> yes, to watch the capsizing
> of women and child voices
> whose offense is vertical
> because they refuse to crawl

is this Christmas and manger?
are these our poems pure white?
are these our poems deep black?
this the summation of poems?

VI

> what right have I to denounce
> while shooting with your own guns?
> or healing with your own hands?
> I freeze and starve for us all

If I could find a kingdom
between midday and midnight
I would go forth and proclaim
my mixed blood to the core

> for I choose the you-in-me
> without color or passport
> they say we all long for God
> and we are all forgiven

VII

si tu venais de toi-même
en ce lieu contradictoire
essayer le rêve amer
des limites solaires

savoir le point de lumière
l'équateur en vérité
n'avoir plus besoin de mer
pour receler tes départs

si tu venais sans colère
au lieu du refus
ouvrir tes yeux à la pluie
te laver à fendre corps

enfin une dernière fois
mettre tes pas dans les pas
de la seule présence en toi
un homme à grandeur de l'homme

mon amour rendu possible
est signé de votre absence
je n'ai plus besoin d'hier
pour être aujourd'hui debout

les manèges de la mer
ne sont plus manèges fous
il fallait parler plus haut
que le sort en dérision . . .

VII

happen you come on your own
to this contradicted place
to embrace the bitter dream
of the solar boundaries

discover the point of light
which is the true equator
having no need of the sea
to conceal your departures

happen you come without wrath
to this place of denial
open your eyes to the rain
lave the body till it splits

at last, for a final time
adjust your steps to the steps
of the sole presence in you:
a man the size of a man

my love may only exist
when endorsed by your absence
I no longer need the past
to stand up in the present

the carousels of the sea
are not mad carousels now
I had to silence my fate
with this, my derisive voice.

Race Relations

I sang in the sun
of my white oasis
as you broke stone

Then I sang and paraded
for the distant martyrs
loving the unknown

They lay still in the sun
of Sharpeville and Selma
while you broke stone

When you fled tyranny
face down in the street
signing stones with your blood

Far away I fell silent
in my white oasis
ringed with smoke and guns

Martyred in safety
I sighed for lost causes
You bled on   You bled on

Now I recommence singing
in a tentative voice
loving the known

I sing in the sun
and storm of the world
to the breakers of stone

You are sentenced to life
in the guilt of freedom
in the prison of memory

Haunted by brothers
who still break stone
I am sentenced to wait

And our love-hate duet
is drowned by the drum
of the breakers of stone

for D.B.

VI

New China

SHU TING:

A POEM IN SIXTEEN SECTIONS

AND TEN OTHER POEMS

The Singing Flower

> Thanks to your shining
> my agony has a faint halo.

I.

I am already a singing flower
Upon your breast
Stirred by the breeze of your breath
As the moonlit fields are stirred

Cover me, please
With your wide palm
For the time being

II.

Now permit me to dream:
Snow. Huge forest.
Ancient windbell. Slanting tower.
May I ask for a genuine Christmas tree?
Ice-skates on its branches,
Fairy tales, magic flutes,
Fireworks vaunting their ardent fountains.
May I rush through the streets laughing loudly?

III.

What has become of my little basket
Heaped with weeds from my Bumper Crop Allotment?
What has become of my old army canteen?
O those thirsty naps under the scaffolding!
The barrettes I never had a chance to wear.
My English exercises: I LOVE YOU LOVE YOU *
My shadow, stretched or shortened under the street lamp
And my tears
        that flowed so many times, so many times choked back.

And more
And more

* In English in the original

Don't ask me
Why I toss lightly in my dreams.
The past, like a cricket in the corner
Whines in its low, persistent voice.

IV.

Permit me a calm dream
Don't leave me alone
That short street – so short!
We have been walking for years

Permit me a quiet dream
Don't disturb me
Those wheeling crows that pester us –
Pay no attention if your eyes are clear

Permit me a dream of absurdity
Don't laugh at me
Each day, newly green, I walk into your poem
Each evening I return to you, bright rose

Let me have an indecent dream
Tolerate my tyranny
When I say, You're mine, you are mine!
Don't reproach me, beloved . . .
I even confess my eagerness to see
          A thousand waves of passion
          Drown you a thousand times.

V.

When our heads touch
As if we were on a speeding train to the moon
The world falls back with a shriek.
The avalanche, Time, swirls madly
               then plunges to pieces.

When our eyes meet
Our souls are like a painting on a gallery wall:
Watery sunlight spreads in rings
        across our field,
Luring us deeper, deeper,
        into harmony, silence and renewal.

VI.

Just like this
We sit in the darkness, clasping hands
And let the voice of our love, ever old and new
Pierce our hearts.
No need to stir, even though
An emperor is knocking at the door

Nevertheless . . .

VII.

Wait! What is that? What sound
Rouses the scarlet pulsing in my veins?
        Now I am dizzy with love
        On the ever-sober ocean
What is that? Whose will
Forces open the lids of my soul and body
        "You must carry the cross on your back
        Every day, and follow me."

VIII.

The dream, umbrella-shaped, takes off
And flies away, a dandelion gone to seed
In a cratered moonscape.

IX.

Wild plum branch: my passionate love,
You choose the precarious life
On a storm-swept slope
Not the elegant pose in a vase.

Wild swan: my temperament,
You vow to confront winter, unprotected
Even with a bullet wound
Rather than linger in the cage of Spring.

At any rate, my name and my belief
Are entered for the race,
A single runner, to represent my nation.
I have no right to rest.
In the marathon of life
Speed itself is the goal.

X.

Towards heaven
Which will judge me in the end
I lift my head.

Wind may sweep me away
But for my heart I reserve the right
To refuse to be counted among the lucky

XI.

Raise your lamp, my love,
                    and show the way
So that I and my poems may travel far.
Somewhere, beyond this morass, an ideal bell
Rings in the soft night.
Villages, towns, swarm into my arms:
                    lights flicker and burn.

Let my poems travel with me,
But the tentacles of highways signal: do not pass!
Still I may walk through the fields
Guided by flowers.

XII.

I walk to the square through the zig-zag streets, back
To the pumpkin shack I guarded, the work in barley fields,
                    deep in the desert (of exile).
Life never stops testing me.
On one side, the laurel wreath, the heavy yoke on the other.
But no one knows I am still that stupid girl
                    bad at mathematics.
No matter how the great chorus seems to drown me,
You will hear my singular voice.

XIII.

Still I stand
Intrepid, proud, younger than ever!
The bitter storm deep in my heart
But sunshine on my forehead:
My bright, transparent yellow skin
My clean, luxuriant black hair!

Mother China
This daughter requires a new name,
She who comes at your call.

XIV.

So call me your birch sapling,
Your little blue star, Mother.
If the bullet comes
Let it strike me first.

I shall slide to the ground from your shoulder
Smiling, with clear eyes.
No tears. Red flowers in the grass.
Blood flaming on its crest.

XV.

My lover, when that time comes
Don't weep
Though there is no one
                    who flings up her pastel skirts
                    who comes through the narrow alley
                    where cicadas sing like the rain
                    to knock at your stained-glass window.
Then there will be no wicked hand
                    to make the alarm clock ring
                    saying angrily, "On your mark!
                    Time to get back to work!"
But don't make a statue of me
On a jade pedestal
And never, to the sound of a lone guitar,
Turn back the calendar, page by page.

XVI.

Your post
Is beneath the banner.
The ideal makes pain bright.
This is the final word
I asked the olive tree
To pass to you.

To find me
Follow the pigeons.
Come in the morning.
I'll be in the hearts
Of women and men.
There you'll find
                    your singing flower.

Bits of Reminiscence

A toppled wine-cup,
A stone path floating beneath the moon
Where the grass was trampled:
One azalea branch left lying there . . .

Eucalyptus trees begin to spin
In a collage of stars
As I sit on the rusted anchor,
The dizzy sky reflected in my eyes.

A book held up to shut out candelight;
Fingers lightly in your mouth;
In the fragile cup of silence
A dream, half-illumined, half-obscure.

Unexpected Meeting

Suddenly the phoenix trees stop swaying,
The sound of bicycle bells is suspended
And the earth rolls back
To that night ten years ago.

Now the phoenix trees begin to sway again.
Flower-petals are ground beneath the wheels
To fling their perfume through the pulsing streets.
The heaven-light of memory blends
With the sight of you.

Perhaps nothing happened. I didn't see you at all:
Hallucination caused by this familiar road.
But even if it did,
I'm used to not shedding tears.

Missing You

A multi-colored chart without a boundary;
An equation chalked on the board, with no solution;
A one-stringed lyre that tells the beads of rain;
A pair of useless oars that never cross the water.

Waiting buds in suspended animation;
The setting sun is watching from a distance.
Though in my mind there may be an enormous ocean,
What emerges is the sum: a pair of tears.

Yes, from these vistas, from these depths,
Only this.

"?.!"

It's true, then,
That you will wait for me
Till I've sowed all the seeds in my morning basket,
Till I've chased home the errant bees of afternoon,
Till the oil lamps or torches of evening have been lit
In the windows of the junks, the shacks, the factories.
Till I have perused them all, both bright and dim,
                and communed with minds both bright and dim;
Till the highway becomes a song,
Till love emerges in the sunshine,
Till the silver river in the sky
                washes us apart,
You will still be waiting patiently,
Trying to tie up your trusty raft.

It's true, then,
That you will never change
When my soft hands are chapped
                and my cheeks have faded,
And my reed flute is stained with blood,
And the snow will never melt again?
Even if, whips on my back, I face the abyss,
Even if dark overtakes me before I reach dawn
                and the earth and I sink together
With no time to send you a message dove,
Will your patience, your loyalty
Be my only reward
For the sacrifices I have made?

Now let them fire on me
While I walk calmly towards you
                across open ground;
To you, to you,
As the wind blows through my long hair.
I am a lily in your storm.

To the Oak

If I love you
I won't imitate the morning glory
Borrowing your high branches to display myself;
If I love you
I won't imitate those infatuated birds
Who repeat their monotonous flattery to the foliage,
Nor the fountain
With its solace of cool waters;
I won't even be those background vistas
That serve to make you more majestic.
Not even sunshine,
Not even spring rain,
No, none of these!
I would like to be a kapok tree
Standing beside you as an equal,
Our roots touching underground,
Our leaves touching in the clouds;
And with every gust of wind
We would bow to one another.
But no one else
Understands our language;
You have your branches
Like daggers or swords
While my big red flowers
Are heavy sighs.
Though it seems we are separated forever
We are eternally together.
This is great love,
This is fidelity.
Love –
Not only for your splendid trunk
But also for the earth you stand on.

To ————————

I pitied you
Beside the gunwale washed by moonlight
Along the rain-spotted way;
Back hunched, hands tucked in sleeves
As if afraid of the cold,
You carefully concealed your thoughts,
But failed to notice
My slow steps
As I walked beside you.
If you were a flame
I would have wished to be the charcoal
To nourish you
But I didn't dare.

Now I rejoice
In the light at your window at midnight,
At the sight of your back bent over your books.
Now you confide in me,
Saying the spring flood
Is brimming over your banks again.
But you neglect to ask
What is in my thoughts each night
When I walk beneath your windows.
If you are a tree
I am the soil.
I want so much to remind you
But I don't dare.

When You Come Past My Window

When you come past my window
Bless me
For my light still burns

As the light was burning
In the night dense with darkness
Like the fisherman's light afloat.
You could say that my little shack
Was a canoe swept away in the storm
But it still hasn't overturned.
My light still burns.

My light still burns.
My silhouette against the curtain
Is the shape of an aging man
With no ardent gestures left,
With a back more bent than it was.
But you know that my heart is not old
For my light still burns.

My light still burns
In response to greetings from every quarter,
With a love hot as an ember
My light still burns
Still fueled with an imperious pride
Contemptuous of coercion, open or disguised.
O how long has it burned with this clear flame?
Since you began to understand me.
My light still burns.

My light still burns.
Bless me
When you come past my window.

Returning Home

Too many echoes
In the wind tonight!
Pine-soughs, fire-flies, lights
                in the village power-plant,
All recalling a distant dream.
Memory: a rickety wooden bridge barely spanning
                the river of time . . .
Is the moon still laughing down the stone steps?
My heart quivers with apprehension.

                Don't remember! Don't remember!
                The wandering feet grow weary.
                Rest your head on the mountain's shoulder.

Having walked far and far,
Yet you find yourself in the same place.
Pure eyes like rising stars
Shine on me as they did a decade ago
(When I was full of hope):
You had only to reach out your hand
And the golden apple would drop into it.
Once the turmoil of the blood
Fell like a brilliant revelation on the soul.
Now it's no longer true, no longer true:
Youth's image recedes through a forest of obligations,
Headed for oblivion.

Perhaps . . .

for the loneliness of an author

Perhaps these thoughts of ours
            will never find an audience
Perhaps the mistaken road
            will end in a mistake
Perhaps the lamps we light one at a time
            will be blown out, one at a time
Perhaps the candles of our lives will gutter out
            without lighting a fire to warm us.

Perhaps when all the tears have been shed
            the earth will be more fertile
Perhaps when we sing praises to the sun
            the sun will praise us in return
Perhaps these heavy burdens
            will strengthen our philosophy
Perhaps when we weep for those in misery
            we must be silent about miseries of our own

Perhaps
Because of our irresistible sense of mission
We have no choice

Brother, I Am Here

Coolness, like the evening tide,
Covers, one by one, the steps of the twisting trail
And slips into your heart.
You sit on the threshold
Of the dismal shack that squats behind you.
Like birds, leaves drift from the locust trees
And little moon-coins float
On the ripple of waves.

You belonged to the sun, the prairie,
The dikes, the world of amorous jewel-black eyes.
Then you belonged to the hurricane,
To the route, the torches, the arms
Supporting each other.
Soldier, your life was plangent as a bell
Shaking the shadows from the human heart.

Now the wind steals away with alien steps;
It refuses to believe
That you are melancholy still.

But I am with you, Brother,
And the newsstand, the park benches, the apple-cores
Revive in your recollection
With smiles and lamps and delicate rhythms.

Then they glide away on the lines of the writing paper.

Only when the night wind
Shifts the direction of your thoughts,
Only when that trumpet of yours
Is suddenly silent, craving echoes,
I shall be back (with hope alive)
Calmly at your side, to say
Brother, I am here.

Born in Spokane, Washington, Carolyn Kizer was educated at Sarah Lawrence College and was a Fellow of the Chinese Government in Comparative Literature at Columbia University and subsequently lived in Nationalist China for a year.

In 1959, she founded *Poetry Northwest* and served as its editor until 1965. From 1966 to 1970, she served as the first Director of the Literature Program at the National Endowment for the Arts. She has been poet-in-residence at Columbia University, Stanford University, and Princeton University, among many others.

In 1985, Kizer received an Award from the American Academy and Institute of Arts and Letters. She also received the Pulitzer Prize for Poetry in 1985 for *Yin* (BOA Editions, 1984). In September of 1988, Kizer received the Theodore Roethke Memorial Foundation Poetry Award (Saginaw, Michigan).

Her other books include *The Ungrateful Garden* (1961), *Knock Upon Silence* (1965), *Midnight Was My Cry* (1971), *Mermaids in the Basement* (Copper Canyon Press, 1984), and *The Nearness of You* (Copper Canyon Press, 1986).

She makes her home in Sonoma, California, with her spouse, John Marshall Woodbridge.